WRITING HOME

First published in 2019 by
The Dedalus Press
13 Moyclare Road
Baldoyle
Dublin D13 K1C2
Ireland

www.**dedaluspress**.com

ISBN 978 1 910251 60 7 (paperback)
ISBN 978 1 910251 61 4 (hardback)

Dedalus Press titles are available in Ireland
from Argosy Books (www.argosybooks.ie) and in the UK
from Inpress Books (www.inpressbooks.co.uk).
Printed in Ireland by Digital Print Dynamics.

Cover image: detail of 'Parallel world 29052017',
80 x 80 cm acrylic on canvas, 2017,
by Anna Hryniewicz *(www.annahryniewicz.com)*
by kind permission of the artist.

The Dedalus Press receives financial assistance from
The Arts Council / An Chomhairle Ealaíon.

WRITING HOME

The 'New Irish' Poets

EDITED BY

Pat Boran

&

Chiamaka Enyi-Amadi

INTRODUCTION BY

Pat Boran

DEDALUS PRESS

ACKNOWLEDGEMENTS and THANKS

The publishers and respective authors would like to thank the editors of the following in which a number of the poems gathered here, or versions of them, originally appeared:

CHIAMAKA ENYI-AMADI – The opening line of 'Where' is taken from 'One Hundred Love Sonnets: XVII' by Pablo Neruda, from *The Essential Neruda: Selected Poems,* edited by Mark Eisner (City Lights Books, 2004); BENJAMIN KEATINGE – 'Passover' and 'A Postcard from FYROM' appeared in *Agenda*, Ekphrastic issue, vol 52, nos 3–4, June 2019; EMMA MUST – 'Cycling to IKEA' appeared in *The Tangerine*, Issue 2, Spring 2017; BOGUSIA WARDEIN – 'From the West Coast' was originally published in *THE SHOp* and 'I Consider My Home Planet' in *Crannóg Magazine;* NIDHI ZAK/ARIA EIPE – 'Ama de Casa' first appeared in *Right Hand Pointing*, Issue 132, May, 2019 while 'Tres(s)pass' was first published as ചുംബനം by *Splonk: The Irish for Flash*, Issue 1, May, 2019.

Special thanks to our friend and neighbour at Dedalus, the multi-talented Anna Hryniewicz, for kind permission to feature her painting 'Parallel world 29052017' on the cover of this book. For more of Anna's work, see *annahryniewicz.com*.

Contents

⤳

INTRODUCTION
'Always Home' – Pat Boran / xiii

⤳

SANA AL BURAIKY
The Girls at the Café / 1
Tree Sounds / 2
Sleepover / 3
Beginnings / 3

ALI BRACKEN ZIAD
3rd November / 5

LYNN CALDWELL
Blanket / 7
The Road Out / 8
In Your Own Dreamtime / 9

POLINA COSGRAVE
Surnames / 10
Say Yes / 10
What You Call Your Nose / 11
Dog I Can't Keep / 11
Ulysses Loses Identity / 12
Stasis / 13
I Told You With My Body / 14
My Name Is / 15

JONATHAN C. CREASY
Notes for a Film / 18

CURT CURTIN
The Lesson / 22
Katie and the Italians / 22

CHIAMAKA ENYI-AMADI
Where / 24
When / 26
How / 28
Dismantling / 29
Women and Other Flowers / 30

AGNIESZKA FILIPEK
All the Souvenirs / 32
Examination of Conscience / 33
Storm / 34
Swan / 34
Light / 35

VIVIANA FIORENTINO
Landing / 36
Currents / 37
Between the Teeth / 37
Roses / 38
An Encounter / 39
Sea-faring / 39

EILISH FISHER
Candle-making at Winter Solstice / 41

EWA FORNAL
Poland / 42

NICOLA GEDDES
After September / 45
Kitchen / 46
Native / 47

Skin / 48
Sound Sleep / 49
Voyager / 50

CHARLEEN HURTUBISE
The Burren / 52
Tornado Siren / 53

CHRIS JONES
Hands / 54
The Green Buddha / 55

KAYSSIE KANDIWA
Mwana WeZuva *(The Child of The Sun)* / 57
Mwana WeVhu *(The Child of the Earth)* / 58
Mwana WeMvura *(The Child of the Water)* / 59
Mwana WaMai *(The Mother's Child)* / 59

NITHY KASA
Accents / 60

BENJAMIN KEATINGE
Passover / 61
A Postcard from FYROM / 62
Borderland / 63

SHANNON KUTA KELLY
In Flight / 64
Upon Arrival in Dublin / 66
Bus to Clonee / 67

SUZZANNA MATTHEWS
Resting, at St. Stephen's Green / 68
Teaching English, at Spencer Dock / 69

JAKI McCARRICK
Camomile / 72
Sanatogen Wine / 73
Kathy in the Kitchen / 74
Home Ground / 75
Midnight in Cricklewood / 75
Shoe Story / 76
The Architect / 76

RAQUEL McKEE
Resilience / 83

VICTORIA MELKOVSKA
Rooted / 86
Boy in a Blue T-Shirt / 87
The Back Door / 87
Two Letters / 90

RAFAEL MENDES
after the james larkin house shooting / 93
on o'connell bridge / 93
32 kg suitcase / 93
staring at stars / 94
dart workers / 95
a beauty / 95
historian / 96
east wall road / 97
são paulo / 98

JULIANA MENEZES
Layers of Me / 100

SHAIYON MERKEL
My Tagore Song / 102
Holi / 103
'Tantra' / 104

NITA MISHRA
I Miss / 105

YAMEEMA MITHA
from A Pakistani Immigrant in Ireland / 107

BRUNO MORANDO
In Smithfield / 109

ELIZABETH MURTOUGH
Some Harvest / 110
Animal Dreams / 111
Southwest Circles / 112

EMMA MUST
After Ophelia / 114
Cycling to IKEA / 115

CHANDRIKA NARAYANAN-MOHAN
Brexit Blues / 117
The 10.35 from Belfast Central to Dublin Connolly / 118
Plane / Train / 119
The Train to Dún Laoghaire / 120
You City, You Boyfriend / 121

GIULIANO NISTRI
Your native home / 123
Kythira / 124
Rented / 125

LIANNE O'HARA
Bench / 127

ART Ó SÚILLEABHÁIN
The Soldier's Rock / 129
Black Love / 130

VIOREL PLOEŞTEANU
snowing in Dublin / 132
your thought / 133
collect call / 133

THEIA PRESADĂ
To all my friends from Sunday Market / 135

MICHAEL RAY
A visitor / 137
Antlers / 138
Foreign rain / 139
Opening a field / 139
Still life / 140
No place home / 141

NATASHA REMOUNDOU
The Dialect of Water / 143

MILENA RYTELEWSKA
Foreigner / 151
First Trip. Drunk Ferry / 152

SIMONE SAV
The Song of the Bird that Does Not Belong / 153
What got left behind / 153
If Insults Were for Sale / 154
Irish Mass / 155
The Present / 156

EDUARD SCHMIDT-ZORNER
Uncompleted CV of a Migrant / 158

EVGENY SHTORN
from Translating Myself / 160

DORINA ŞIŞU
Today you go again … / 163
let's say / 164
on the coast of Ireland / 166

CSILLA TOLDY
Flotsam memories / 167

ERIKO TSUGAWA-MADDEN
Page Turner / 170
Apache / 170
Fr. Bradley / 171
Mother died yesterday / 172

BOGUSIA WARDEIN
From the West Coast / 174
I Consider My Home Planet / 175

CHRISTIAN WETHERED
Woodcote / 177
Bray / 177
You Were Born in an Ark / 178

LANDA WO
On the hill, my tomb, marine cemetery / 179

NIDHI ZAK/ARIA EIPE
Tres(s)pass / 180
Hard Border / 180
Ama de Casa / 182
C'est poésie / 183

INTRODUCTION

– ALWAYS HOME –

PAT BORAN

'Where are we going? Always home.'
— *Novalis, 18th century German poet and philosopher*

'**H**OME' IS AMONG the most emotive words there is. It refers to the place we come from, the place we first became ourselves; it seems to describe an intimate part of us. Just as many fairytales end with the protagonists (often children) making it, against all odds, back home, so too do the words 'home', 'safety' and 'security' seem at first glance almost interchangeable.

If our own times teach us anything, however, it is that not everyone shares in the same lucky experience.

For such an apparently innocuous word, it's remarkable that 'home' so regularly features in the most contentious debates of our age. From the international refugee crisis to Trump's xenophobic dream-wall; from the relationship between local action and climate change to the shame of people sleeping on our streets, this most innocent-seeming word seems to conjure a battleground for the rights and freedoms of future generations.

Of course people travel for all sorts of reasons – study, work and simple curiosity among them. Many of us at some point choose to live elsewhere for an extended period, to make our (temporary) homes elsewhere, finding in 'foreign lands' things that will enrich our lives when we arrive 'back home'. Indeed for workers in the IT, banking and related sectors, this has almost become the norm.

For others, however, that outward journey is undertaken with considerable reluctance, resulting in feelings of displacement and loss that geographical distance alone cannot explain. One thinks, for instance, of a generation of Irish labourers marooned in mainland Britain as if they had been shipwrecked on the far side of the world. Always dreaming of home.

Perhaps we need to make a distinction between 'homeland' and 'home', the former designating a given, historical fact, the latter a place we continuously reimagine and refine. And for those who never enjoyed safety or understanding in their 'homelands' or 'first homes', the journey outwards may be even more difficult, the task that lies ahead of them all the more daunting.

For some writers, all of these jostling meanings and connotations of the word 'home' sit down to join them whenever a pen is picked up or a computer is switched on. The magnetic attraction and the simultaneous resistance of the word is one of the reasons why, for so many, the exploration of 'home' is one of the first steps into a writing life. And so, the dual sense of delight and trepidation is everywhere in these poems.

Having settled on The 'New Irish' Poets as the subtitle for this gathering, I confess to remaining somewhat uneasy about it as a label. Labels don't do much for poetry, or for art in general. Impressionism, Cubism, Neo-Expressionism … The most distinguished practitioners push beyond the limitation of labels to make something new. For instance, we might reasonably ask: When do the 'New Irish' become the 'Old Irish' or just the 'Irish', without any need for qualification? That said, a little unease is not unusual (or entirely useless) at the start of a journey. If nothing else, it quickens the heartbeat and ensures that we pay attention.

As a boy I was much entertained by the suggestion that my surname might have a somewhat exotic origin. An uncle who served as a missionary in Kenya imagined he'd found a meaningful link with the well-known Boran people of that country (footnoted, to my delight, in Alex Haley's bestselling novel *Roots,* an international *cause célèbre* at that time.)

Years later, discovering that the name was also common in Turkey, Thailand and a number of other places, I realised that its simple two-syllable form might be basic to any number of languages, and my bubble was burst. Even so, that 'African connection' implanted in my adolescent self the notion that we are all from somewhere else – a notion which, when we think on a scale of more than a few generations, is these days demonstrably true. It is not only politics or commerce but even science itself that reminds us how much more complex and interesting is the real story of who we are and where we come from.

Nowadays when I think of the phrase 'New Irish', I think first of my Sicilian wife of almost twenty years, and then of my two Sicilian-born, Dublin-raised, trilingual sons. Despite my own immersion in Irish culture (or at least in the English language part of it), ours is, statistically speaking, a 'New Irish' family unit; and, like that of our Bosnian, Polish and Tunisian neighbours, among others, our story too is part of the longer narrative of ongoing change.

⁓

At the Dedalus Press, we have long been committed to international writing and writing in translation and proud of our reputaton as 'one of the most outward-looking poetry publishers in Ireland and the UK' (UNESCO.org). A significant step on our own journey was the publication in 2010 of the anthology *Landing Places: Immigrant Poets in Ireland,* edited by Eva Bourke and Borbála Faragó, in part a response to the widespread changes in Ireland of the so-called Celtic Tiger years. Where that book presented the general observations of the writers gathered therein (many of whom had already or have since gone on to publish poetry collections of their own), for the present volume we thought to focus on writers not yet established in English, and to prompt them to respond to our general theme of 'home', mindful that a description of place is both a record of ongoing change and a rudimentary self-portrait of the artist.

It has been my pleasure to work with Chiamaka Enyi-Amadi in selecting the poems for this volume. Though her own experience as a young, female, Nigerian-born, Irish-bred writer is clearly very different to mine, we were both pleased to note how much agreement there was between our core selections. Reading 'blindly' is a liberating and often an illuminating experience, not least when, after the selection process is complete, the identities of the writers are revealed.

Though they are presented as a unit here, this anthology hopes to recognise the differences as well as the similarities among its contributors. A list of these poets' countries of origin ranges from Angola to Zimbabwe (with Brazil, Canada, the Democratic Republic of the Congo, England, Germany, Hungary, Italy, Japan … in between). But to list them like that is to create a false sense that these writers in some way 'represent' their countries of origin, like the competitors in some kind of International Poetry Games.

Instead it might be better to think of them in three general groups. Here are poets who were born 'elsewhere' and now make their life – or part of their life – here in Ireland (poets whose kitchens smell of the herbs and imported ingredients of other lands, one might say). Here too are poets who were born here but who dream in the culture or language of another place, inheritors of their parents' aspirations and memories. And here too are a small number of poets born and perhaps raised in this country, but who have subsequently spent enough time outside of it that, sometimes, it too seems like an 'elsewhere' to them now.

So what, then, is the true nature of home? How do we distinguish between the place we wish to imagine into being and the one from which we have emerged? One thing is sure, we never see our home place as clearly as when we see it in the company of a stranger, a visitor or new arrival who notices and questions the things that, for us, have long since become invisible. In that sense, this anthology is not just about the journey and experience of these fifty-one 'New Irish' poets; it is also about the meaning of 'home' itself.

Not everything we find in these pages will be welcome or positive. A number of the poets describe incidents of casual, or less than casual, xenophobia or outright racism, certainly not unique to Ireland (and perhaps less common here than in some jurisdictions), but troubling nonetheless. Visitors to our Emerald Isle have often struggled to balance the warmth of the *céad míle fáilte,* or 'one hundred thousand welcomes', with that curious first question many outsiders face, 'How long are you here for?' which sometimes translates as, 'And when are you going back?' Could it be that even the fabled Irish welcome is not always as genuine as it might appear.

Reading through an anthology such as this, one imagines a possible mirror volume – a compilation of poems by the generation of Irish-born poets now making their lives and homes overseas. The truth is that the movement of people (out of necessity, opportunity or simple curiosity) is intrinsic to our species and certainly to our times. But that particular volume is a project for another day.

For now, with *Writing Home: The 'New Irish' Poets,* we celebrate external influence and fresh perspectives; we celebrate not just new and emerging voices but new linguistic and cultural threads being woven into the fabric of Irish life. More than anything, we celebrate 'arrival' itself, in a country that is perhaps more used to commemorating departure and loss. And, so long as writing continues to be supported, published and championed here, we believe we have reason yet to be proud of this place we call our 'writing home'.

– 20 August 2019
Baldoyle (from *Báile dubh-ghall,*
the town of the dark-haired foreigner)

Sana Al Buraiky

Sana Al Buraiky is a poet from Qatif, Saudi Arabia. She is a student at University College Dublin. Her poetry considers themes of youth, nostalgia & change, and has been published in UCD English & Literary Society's Caveat Lector. She has been living and studying in Ireland since 2015.

The Girls at the Café

doused in perfume & family legacy
mothers' gold & daddy issues
scents mistaken for change

I don't know their names – we don't talk
in this era of cinema
in the mirror, they get fixed up
hands combing hair down to the waist

last time I remember
they whispered   *such a waste*
but the ears in the walls have fallen off
scotopic vision still adjusting
out on the balcony
Marlboros on the table

                they catch a light

Tree Sounds

Our Ziziphus spina-christi's got thorns
so do the Manila tamarinds, semi-evergreen
with their winded plumpness of
red & green fuzz but they don't
prick Abu Alhusain's hands

green thumbs over the nozzle of
the garden hose, he sprays
parched tree trunks
now turned prosperous on
inhospitable grounds

he lays geranium beds in the earth
bare-grips weeds that don't belong
sickle hacking away, glass jars overflow
with black beetles from
where he stands

beat-up plastic two-litre bottle, it lights up like
an emerald filled to the brim
all the gardeners share water
poured arm's-length
into their mouths

the sun does not shy away
mornings through afternoons
sweat-drenched he shoos a
cat cooling itself belly flat
to the dampened land

season to season
this garden as much his
as it is ours

Sleepover

The girls get their hair tied up
in pyjamas,
nail-polished biters
you can peel off their skin
without getting under it

the girls sit with their knees bent
faces anchored down by
red lipstick frowns –
they look so picturesque

but that's the kind of thing
you're not supposed to say
so I don't
I don't say anything
to the sad girls
with their knees bent

Beginnings

The sky's above us, we assume
though we can't see
most of it

countdown under green
fluorescence
from the unpainted garage
Lujain sits on cracked marble steps
goddess of this night

across a dead genus of trees

that grew much earlier than we did
here, the smell of cheap coal burns
our bronchi
(maybe it was something else?)

neighbourhood rascals' voice
aah!
a disagreement outside
likely unresolved
strays approach & meow
peering over the fence
Lujain burns a finger, flipping
a burger patty to the ground

purrs with his prize
content, and so are we

laugh –
it's New Year's after all

Ali Bracken Ziad

Irish-Iraqi Ali Bracken Ziad is currently working on a debut chapbook entitled *Place and People Without*. He has been published in *Feasta, Ó Bhéal's Five Word Anthology, Spoken Worlds: Exhaling Ink, The Evening Echo* and *The Quarryman*. He was awarded the Eoin Murray Memorial Scholarship in Creative Writing in 2018, holds a BA (Hons) in English from University College Cork, and is currently studying law at UCC.

3ʳᵈ November

One hundred years on and change is still in question,
Torn between Heaney, Ní Chuilleanáin,
James Joyce and Derek Mahon.
For what reason have the funerals emigrated from my brain
     to the world,
And why has the government of my tongue unfurled.

Who are the mushrooms that are locked in our shed,
Where nobody cares about the living, or the dead.
Why can't we give up Ithaca and the furrows in its face,
Don't worry, we are sand, washed without a trace.

It feels like yesterday that the Dunnes Stores Girls refused to
     stock Israeli product,
And Google Maps still listed Palestine as a nation not a
     construct.
It feels like yesterday that the Greeks turned Babylon into
     Athens

And Enheduanna into Homer
And falsafa into philosophos
And criticism into crime.

It feels like yesterday that the singers said such things as:
Don't fight between a rock and a hard place
Don't turn life into a universal form of catch-twenty-two
Don't get so angry when the soldiers kill your brother and rape
    your mother
Don't run away now we need you to fight
Don't forget about the big other
That turns Zeus into El Shadai into God into Allah into
    das Übermensch.
Don't forget that tools may change but trends and iterations do not.

So be ready,
And don't forget to read every writer-you-love's enemy.
Do not usurp your peace,
If time is seasonal where are we.
But sing.

It feels like yesterday
Today
It feels like yesterday.

Lynn Caldwell

Lynn Caldwell is a Canadian who has watched the changing faces of Ireland for more than 25 years. Her work has been published in *The Irish Times, FLARE, The Antigonish Review* and *Proem Canada,* and has featured on RTÉ's *Sunday Miscellany.* She was a runner-up in Aesthetica's Creative Writing Award 2017, and has a BA in creative writing from the University of Victoria, Canada.

Blanket

I.

A gift, soft fleece in tones of grey and black,
sewn by a cousin,
its snug layers feeling like family,
I tuck this blanket around
my boy-manchild's long body
as I have done since his legs
hardly reached the middle of the bed.
And I think
if we were to flee in the night,
this is one thing I would take.
It folds into a pillow, is warm,
comforting, has memories and love
stitched around the pocket.
I briefly see us huddled
somewhere dark and cold
dangerously desperate.
I don't hold onto this picture.

II.

If you have to run for your life
take any cash you have,
all the documents you can find,
your phone, with/without charger,
shoes, if you can put them on quick enough,
a map in your head of escape routes.
Pull each of your family from the corners
they slouch in, back from the fridge
where they stand,
run, your hands digging into their wrists,
your breath hot on their cheeks,
Come on! Run!
Go without a thought
of your favourite mug, a memory stick of photos,
the cards on the mantle.
Hope the Red Cross has food packs, blankets, tents.
Bring only those things
that get you past borders, onto boats and planes,
away from the panic of what once was your home,
your bed, your body stretching to fill the warm spaces,
those things that say who we are,
knowing nothing about us.

The Road Out

How was I to know the road out
would be the road back?
Home itself ephemeral –
found in the scent of boxwood,
a drift of cherry leaves,
the odd snowflake,
a hand to hold.

How was I to know you
would give the best directions,
your compass aligned to my true north?
Always ready
to go off road with me,
to make tracks where no one should go.

My own terrain is changed;
knowing the map of your body helps.
I have memorised lines and contours;
I could read it with my eyes closed.
You are good at reading the road,
always remembering the way back.

In Your Own Dreamtime

Somewhere between creation and birth
in your own dreamtime
your journey outward began.
Before you ever saw the light of day, the sun rose, set on you
on three continents.
You crossed oceans once, twice, four times.
You ask *where* before *why,*
your fingers tracing a river on a map,
following the flow from source to sea.
Lines of latitude mark your space.
You reach to grasp poles, stretch toward the equator.
There's no holding you back.
I can see the open road in your eyes.

Polina Cosgrave

Polina Cosgrave was born in Volgograd, Russia. Her poetry in Russian was featured on national radio and TV in 2015. She came to Ireland in 2016 and graduated from the American College Dublin with an MFA in Creative Writing. Her work in both Russian and English has been published in journals and anthologies. She is a member of the New Irish Communities workshop at the Irish Writers Centre.

Surnames

I'm a Russian girl with an Irish surname,
Who was a Russian girl with a Jewish surname,
Who was a Russian girl with a Russian surname
Who once spent nine months in a belly of
An Armenian girl with a Russian surname.
All these surnames
I can neither acknowledge nor return,
each opening or eclipsing the other
like a Russian doll.

Say Yes

I love you in the mornings, as sunlight passes through clouds making them shine from the inside. I want to marry the lemon colour of your sky. You're full of gold, Ireland. Say Yes.

I love you when you're sad and grumpy, and I can hear the rain playing war drums on the roof and the wind is about to knock down the walls. You're full of power, Ireland. Say Yes.

I love you when you're cold as stone, when you teach me how to warm the room with my voice. I love you when you sparkle with laughter, when you remind me that seriousness kills poetry.

Nobody ever talked to me the way you do, Ireland. I love what you did to the English language, for in your mouth it is the language of humour and seduction.

I know you've been through a lot, and I have come to tell you you're beautiful and the best is yet to come. I promise to be true to you in good times and in bad. You are my perfect mirror that shows I can be so much more. You're full of life, Ireland. Say Yes.

What You Call Your Nose

Volgograd smells like T-34, lilac and lace,
Saint Petersburg smells like granite and grace,
Moscow smells like red flowers, gold and cement,
Dublin smells like blood and salt,
As for me, I smell of letters never sent,
As for you, you smell of stories never told.

Dog I Can't Keep

First language is a dog I can't keep anymore
Barking in the back of my mind.
Stay, I command.
But it goes wherever it pleases,
Reminding me who is the real owner here.
Its growling is so powerful that all other sounds get lost in it.
Your bites leave no scars anymore, I say.
I'll find you a new home, I say.
It grins.

First find yourself one.
Its jaws are closing around my neck.

Ulysses Loses Identity

When a local mistakes your oar
For a fan that winnows the grain
You won't have to search anymore,
May your spirit abandon pain.
Yes, the locals will take your oar
For an artless winnowing fan!
But until you have reached that shore
You're no one in a foreign land.
All the words you mumble, they crush
As the waves embracing the stone
All you see is a dumb mirage
Trapped and wrapped in the shadow zone
Should you ask? Do you have a right
For a shelter you've craved and missed?
There's no refuge for you tonight,
And the sky no longer exists.
There's no sky, in a strange delight
You still feel that the stars are there
Just bled grey, they bled black and white
There's no roof: all you do is stare.
There's no roof, yet there is a hope
For a gentle and warming flame
For a house you can call your home
For the people to say your name
Yes, some man will mistake your oar
For a winnowing fan one day
And you'll know: it's the end of war
And you'll know: there a place to stay.

Stasis

Green is the heart, I promise.
Don't bother digging in,
I swear, my heart is green.
You won't believe me, no.
Come on, then, grab a shovel.
And cut right here, I'll show you.
My heart is full of grass,
I swear by all the insects that hide inside my body,
By bugs and worms and tickling little ants.
They grow right through the heart
Towards the sunshine,
Those piercing blades of grass.
Green is the heart,
And grey, the blood.
You won't believe me, no.
My blood is grey, my flesh is stone and clay.
I swear it by the rains
And streams which fill my body,
Which flow into my body,
Those streams that lick my toes.
I am the land,
My mouth is full of soil,
So are the eyes and ears,
Wet is the breath.
Warm is the voice, I promise.
My melting lungs
Are glistening with dew.
The thighs are sweet, I swear.
I'll wait for you.
I'm waiting for you there.

I Told You With My Body

You already know,
I told you with my body.
I want to fight you in every way I can,
Question everything you are:
From your eye colour
To the language you speak.
I want myself to drink from your speech,
Erase the words you write
And explain
That there is no such thing as a personality.
You are as much as an entity
That feels like fire
And a home
At the same time,
But if I'm burning
How will I save my place from the flames?
But you already know,
I told you with my body.
You are new to me
In the way you wear your lips,
In the way you wear my lips.
Could you be real in the story of me?
Like death,
Like drowning,
Like a barfly,
Like a lover,
Like a listener,
Like a passer-by,
Like a foreigner,
Like a memory imprinted between my thighs?
I want to learn
Who you are
And after you change your skin

I'll be there to relearn it.
Then you can question everything I am.
How far will I go to get what I desire?
But we already know,
I said that with my body.
I would trade my dozen jobs
And all the men I kept in my bed
And all the women who kept me wondering what I am made of
For watching the river flow
As you are breathing next to my shoulder.
Can I be real in the story of you?
Would I be more significant
If I disappeared
From web-pages
Immigration offices
People's minds?
Nobody matters.
However,
If you were all I knew about human beings
It would be enough.
I think I've already told you this with my body.

My Name Is

The name of an old man whose head was torn off by a bomb and
    whose body was left on the frozen soil of Stalingrad,
The name of his wife whose body slowly melted in times of
    hunger and cold,
The name of their daughter who carried her wounded child
    through the burning streets,
The name of her husband, who was imprisoned by the country
    he fought for,
The name of their little girl who survived the war and named me,

The name of a little boy that came to rebuild the ruins of the city with one piece of bread in his pocket, which was stolen by a dog,

The name of their son who once bought me a bullfinch in a cage so I could set the bird free,

The name of his great-grandfather who escaped from Nazi camp and got into a Soviet one as a punishment for cooperation with the enemy,

The names of four Armenian siblings who lost their parents to typhus and moved to the devastated Russia to establish a new generation,

The name of their father who had his name engraved on a Nagant revolver,

The name of his wife, Siranush, which means love, the only name that should be given to a woman,

The name of her great-granddaughter, who is the only reason I'm still here,

The name of her younger brother, who's been tortured in the pre-trial detention for six months and the name of what's left of him afterwards,

The name of his cousin, who's been beaten in the army for six hours and the name of what's left of him afterwards,

The name of my cousin, whose heart stopped on New Year's Eve,

The name of my grandfather, whose heart stopped when I touched the Western Wall,

The name of his niece, whose cancer was as blistering as her passion for life,

The name of her nephew, who got a bullet in his head because he was Azerbaijani,

The name of my friend, who never woke up after her 19th birthday,

The name of my friend, who never woke up after her boyfriend threw her out of the window on International Women's Day,

The name of my friend who never woke up after taking a pill,

The name of my lover, whose mind is murdered with drugs and
    depression, who goes into a war against his own madness
    each time he wakes up,
The name of the Unknown Soldier, on whose bones my
    hometown is built.
I am so full of names.
My name is a verb,
My name is to awake,
My name is to destroy,
My name is *cavt tanem*,
'I would take away your pain',
Say it like it's yours.

Jonathan C. Creasy

Jonathan C. Creasy is a writer, musician, broadcaster, and filmmaker based in Dublin. Born and raised in California, he studied music with jazz legends Peter Erskine, Jeff Hamilton and Charlie Haden. Creasy earned a BA Honours and PhD in English Literature from Trinity College Dublin. His work has appeared in *The Irish Times, Poetry Ireland Review, The Stinging Fly, gorse,* and many other publications. He teaches English and Creative Writing in UCD.

Notes for a Film

for Benjamin Alire Sáenz & Angela Kocherga

SCENE I
EXT. Texas borderlands – midday

The picture in my mind is more
than I'll ever be –

the hands, the wall, the kids
desert mountains make

blankets of sky
and thousands of miles away

across too many seas to name
history slouches back against

all this forgotten time.

How do you turn movement
into monuments?

The pictures on your screen are more
than you'll ever see –

the crowd, the face, the land
the terrible truth

you can just about say.

What songs do these winds
carry, and how far

before they scatter out over
brown and white and grey?

I have no doubt that seeing
is believing, yet saying what

it is we see is something
different.

The poet tells us we've
misnamed this place.

What if after all
we've misplaced the names?

The painter says the colours are only
ever approximate –

there is no perfect form
for representation.

Even from outside
you might then be led to wonder

how the brown dead earth
gives life to such

immaculate green.

SCENE II
INT. Dublin public house – late afternoon

Or is it night now over the river's
divide? Take your time here

before you wander –

the other voice, the one you're born with,
sits well in silence,

despite your living on its
confidence and confusion.

Not far from here and not
long ago (things considered)

an accent cut close to the grave

some say all that's over
and some that it's only sleeping

there is one thing I know that
we ought to tell the truth about:

the image on the wall is of a woman
who will never stay silent,

even though you cannot know her name.

Curt Curtin

Born in Boston, Massachusetts, Curt Curtin is a first generation Irish-American poet. Both his parents emigrated from County Kerry, giving him a unique perspective about Irish citizens who relocated to the United States. He has published three chapbooks, had poems published in several journals, and has won several poetry awards. He taught creative writing and college English in the US and is active in the Worcester (MA) Poetry Association.

The Lesson

When I was a boy of seven or nine
my Da taught the closing of doors.
We stood by the kitchen door, he leaning low
and near, his face become the room itself.
He said, 'You turn the knob – like this.'
The rough map of his hand covered everything:
the knob, the vast kitchen where our lesson met,
perhaps the universe where moments went
to be turned and turned until they could be seen
from anywhere. 'You do'ant need to slam.'

Katie and the Italians

I've nothing against them, mind you,
though it was grand when
the neighbourhood was only Irish

and you could tell who it was
was stealing towels off the line.

Italians started moving in
when they ran out of space in
another place to put up shrines,
cement to saint Anthony or Rocco.
They've an awful passion for cement,
using it for steps and porches and
even seats. My John says if many
more move in all the houses
will sink ten feet with the weight.
That's what happened in Venice, he said.

And there's the smell of their cooking.
Sure, it can't be right to be spoiling
good food with garlic and basil.
Myself, I use a spoon or two of salt,
and there's only a nice bit of smell to
boiled potatoes and butter, though
it does get strong when I boil the beef
with cabbage and turnips. At least
they've never complained, though
how would I know with them talking
in their way faster than I can say
the rosary. My John says they put olive oil
on their tongues to make them go fast.

I do say they're very generous people.
The ones next door gave my John a
whole gallon of homemade red wine.
We're not sure what to do with it,
but we thanked them anyway and
gave them a mackerel John caught
down at the docks.

Chiamaka Enyi-Amadi

Chiamaka Enyi-Amadi was born in Lagos, Nigeria and raised in Galway and Dublin. A graduate of UCD with a BA Honours in English and Philosophy, she writes and performs her poetry, most recently at the Mountains to Sea Book Festival and on RTÉ's *Poetry Programme*. Her writing is particularly focused on themes of shifting and marginal identities. She was the 2019 recipient of the Poetry Ireland Access Cúirt Bursary.

Where

> *Home is not where you are born, home is where all your attempts to escape cease – Naguib Mahfouz*

... without knowing how or when, or from where*
I have stopped dreaming of escape from a country

on whose ground I could settle my feet
but not my spirit. I thought my mind had betrayed me

the day I woke wanting to remember each moment
where I feel at home. My memory is a wool blanket,

fraying at the edges, an unreliable garment
barely thick enough to throw over my back

to trap time, smother it safely, keep each moment
Intact, and I can open my time-blanket

whenever I'm in need of spare-keys
or the balm of love-soaked nostalgia. Instead I bookmark

the *NY Times* article '36 Questions That Lead to Love',
mark a Google Calendar date every month for us to brunch

sitting on a high or low olive wood stool
in some high-end or back street cafe

in Dublin mostly or Galway at Doyle's
or Amsterdam or Belfast at Bert's

I sit anywhere, always facing you.
Each time we are old strangers

equipped with questions to connect new dots,
after all we hacked the 'love algorithm' once before.

What are the odds of us
not getting sick of each other.

What are the odds of getting to a place
where all our attempts to escape cease?

Sure you take the piss, keep saying
this kind of carry on will make you end it all,

you'd sooner dig deeper, grimace at some dormant malaise,
bare your sores rather than risk losing your way ...

Your need for 'organised chaos', sneaking scoops
of butter onto your tongue the moment my head is turned,

and my tendency to dissect every situation
if only to keep me sane in this epic guessing game.

... without knowing how or when, or from where
I have stopped dreaming of escape

And began wanting to remember each moment
where I feel at home, with you.

* from a line by Pablo Neruda

When

My mind is weak on isolated detail.
I ask that each book, each song, each supper of yours,

must have a story attached whether it's the first
or last, or I'll struggle to make memory of it –

... goes in one ear then leaks out ...
the other night I went digging in old drawers

reached into my memory box,
I'd kept it all, fourteen months

from the fourteenth day of February
the night you first cooked me dinner

sirloin steak seared
in a pan of melted butter,

toss the button mushrooms to fry
in clear juices, spring onion chopped

without watering your eyes,
bulbs of garlic crushed,

baby potatoes seasoned – bold flavours –
with your mother's many spices.

On a cold evening I wait for you
outside Dún Laoghaire station:

a faded figure rushing through
Autumn drizzle

approaches with a smile, shy, falters,
both of us shielded by the inadequate roof

of the bus shelter. You hand me
red roses, as if we'd dined before.

I pull a gloved hand from my coat pocket
to take them. As we walk towards the house,

dinner warm in the oven waiting to be served,
my fingers stiffen from the chill.

I'd kept it all, crisp red petals
now a dark shade of brown –

stalk and flower pressed
into my journal pages together with

the note you wrote in gratitude
for that copy of Neruda ('*the gift of life,*

that without cease I give you'), once a vibrant thing,
soaking up the scent held to my nostril;

let the petals lick my lips,
brown on top, pink beneath.

How

the harmony of skin
on skin, of flesh meeting

in hunger, in wonder, *i ngrá*
in sweat, tears, blood

between my legs too soon
painting your cotton sheets crimson.

While I sleep it seeps through,
some old part of me steadily

leaving, this time too soon.
I am at a loss, I have no tool

to plug this sudden drip.
This time, I do my one good trick:

turn a site of desire into a pit of despair,
and bury myself in shame and stained sheets.

You wake and reach for me,
the harmony of skin on skin, of flesh

meeting in hunger, in wonder, *i ngrá;*
you feel the sheets, wet, my body in retreat.

You spring up, grabbing towels,
manoeuvre me (half against my will),

wrapping thick white towels around my waist
and between my legs. I have no choice:

I give in, allow my body take centre stage,
announce my pain out loud,

and you reach for me again, the harmony
of skin on skin … my body in distress.

Dismantling

                              you promised home
                              things I want most
reassure me
what is mine
                              for keeping,
                              for dismantling
to start afresh
organic cotton sheets
                              tucked tight
                              no escape
even for me
at least none with ease
                              search Google
                              crawl through carpets
of mud-gold foliage
Dublin streets doubling
                              in Spring, busy boulevards
                              crowded cafés, cinema trips
open-mics, libraries, parks,
ponds; pretend to watch ducks
                              'thoroughly fascinating'
                              turn the world on its head
then tilt back to show off
speckled green neck
                              smug yellow beak
                              smooth as the skin of an apricot

iridescent water-peacock
you have everything to be proud of
                        but you're lonely
                        dependent on daily bread
the company of old and young
if not of blood
                        trap me in the love-bubble
                        wrap me whole, in organic promises,
white-lies, fresh sheets
tucked tight in your arms, tell me your intent
                        when I find it hard
                        to keep steady breaths
in and out, puff out your chest
pretend you sucked the air from my lungs
                        press your cracked lips against mine
                        blow hard, give what is mine
for keeping, for dismantling
return with me to memory
                        a billowing cloud of dust
                        where a childhood home used to be

Women and Other Flowers

Once upon a time a little girl turns eleven and is transformed
into a new EU citizen. But then she spends her first Irish winter
desperate, weeping, her mother shrouding her in a floral duvet,
her stalk-thin, pre-teen body pressed against the radiator in the
hallway of their new house all one frosty night. Shivering, she
clings to its heat, wheezing, a young willow battered by the wind,
needing shelter in an arch of sunshine, ribs aching against

metal ridges, her soft breathing intertwined
with the whistling of something sinister trapped

within, a symphony of shared
corporeal struggle. Attempts at settling, at staying alive

and sentimentality do not suit perennial beings;
there are seasons for such morbid things.

And ever after? – a delicate time,
spent in the trauma of self-

renewal, preparing
to be whole again.

Agnieszka Filipek

Agnieszka Filipek lives in Galway. She writes in both her native tongue Polish and in English, and also translates in these languages. Her work has been published internationally in countries such as Poland, Ireland, India, China, England, Wales, Germany, Bangladesh, Canada and the United States. Recently her poems appeared in *Marble Poetry Magazine, Pale Fire: New Writing on the Moon Anthology* and *Chrysanthemum*. For more, visit *www. agnieszkafilipek.com*

All the Souvenirs

everything tastes better in bed
you whispered in my ear
too many times

I smashed all the souvenirs from the places
you always wanted to visit
shouting out her name

shattered pieces getting deep
into your Persian rug
like knives into flesh

frantically trying to change a hoover bag
and everything else in my life
job flat breakfast cereal

no more take away pizza
from that Italian place
on the corner

we were always forgetting napkins
and you were licking
my fingers

Examination of Conscience

on the edge of yesterday
I stood at the crossroads of my heart
and killed two loves with one stone
God has forgiven me
you would forgive me too

on the edge of today
I forget myself
I cut my hair and shamelessly
put on a white dress
the priest forgives me

on the edge of tomorrow
the sea of sadness
will come under my feet
I will turn my back on memories
God will forgive me

on the edge of life
in a black dress
I will finally
remember
and forgive myself

Storm

I'm crushed, torn
         from the wedding
                  photographs. You're

drenched with rain
         and alcohol and women's
                  perfume. The fairytale

ended and for us there's
         no tomorrow. The doves
                  flew away, their nest

ripped apart. It wasn't
         strong enough to survive
                  the storm. They say

a home is built for two.

Swan

I rub out the sun with an eraser
glue stars onto the sky
cut out the moon from a National Geographic

I arrange lamps
on empty streets
lighting one at your favourite bench

Fallen leaves
rustle under my boots
collected by the wind

A swan swims in the city fountain
I don't know what he's doing here
alone at night

He's nestling his head in feathers
tucking himself
underneath his wings

Light

The church bells sounded in the distance, when I
fell to the ground. The sky was strangely blue,
rainbow sparks danced before my eyes and their
brightness blinded me. Who was I? Where did I

come from? Where was I going? Everything
swirled. Nothing was the same. I took a deep
breath. I swam, floating in a cocoon of light,
without time, without the clock of death. And

suddenly everything was bright in my head,
but everything was so dark around. The truth
spoke through every cell of my body crying
out with tears. For the first time I really opened

my eyes. People, like statues moved in rows,
like on production lines. Their lost dreams
dragging behind them, like beaten dogs afraid
to leave. In the twilight I touched your shoulder,

you didn't look at me, your eyes fixed on your
wallet. I stopped on the island of self–love,
which was big enough only for two feet. I
balanced on one leg, reaching out my hand.

Viviana Fiorentino

Viviana Fiorentino was born in Italy. After obtaining a PhD, she travelled across Europe and then moved to Belfast. In 2017, she left academia to focus on writing while teaching Italian Literature. Since 2018 she has taken part in literature festivals and has been awarded a number of poetry prizes; her poems appear on literature blogs and international magazines. In 2019 she published the poetry collection *In giardino* with Controluna Press and her first novel *Tra mostri ci si ama* with Transeuropa Press.

Landing

i
Sky, you are too big;
Persian Blue –
I cannot know you.

ii
Instead, I call on you, Land;
give me a place to put my feet,
a home for my uncertainty,
a place to doubt.

iii
A place to live.

Currents

This is a shawl of salt and seaweed
against the Atlantic wind
the ocean currents on the sea bed
of my life, your life
a dream, a burnished pearl.

Between the Teeth

We blether, idling, chittering,
time passes,
like ice melting
or something sweet
dissolving in the mouth
yet thickening there between the teeth.

I know the wind
carries more than spores;
chances, places to fall, or settle
and root in moss, like
Chanterelles
in Carraigín or Sphagnum
and others, and yet others …

There is white light in you still
grown from the heart of your
sorrow's seed
hesitant, and latent,
secret as stone.

Roses

In my mind
I can still tend the rose garden
of my childhood –
inside me, as if it is my blood
as if it is serum, pulsing, season
on season.

Back then, at the shore
beach-tar on my feet,
I was a child,
but a space remained,
plump, pink, liminal and pure
between its cloying stain
and the life in me.

Life happens this way –
that even now
when I am at risk of drowning
I close my lips tight
against the pressing saltwater
my head tilting backwards
refusing to breathe in
and I am surfacing, like the call
of oystercatchers
piping after the rain,
a pool of pure joy, or like
Socrates'
swans, full throated and defiant
singing,

> *I have lived.*
> *I have lived.*

An Encounter

You ask me
why is the sky
open and without limits
for swans, for geese, for terns
but not for us.

Here, we cannot even see the
sky;
this room is suffocating,
hot, without windows,
strip lights cast shadows
of our hands across this table.

Like birds
we are trapped
and disorientated
in white light
milling
crying out into the dark.

Left to our own instincts
we could find our way
on cool nights
navigating
with the stars
the coastline
landmarks.

Sea-faring

The horizon is far bigger
than the oceans and rocks

that have troubled me.
The scene fractures
crackling like paint on boats.
The sea has washed everything
where I was swallowed and spat
out
like a doll, drowned and buried in
the sand;
it sought the beach
but now lies broken
and twisted at its very core.

Over there, where the ridge
slumps
I tell you
more flushed scatterings
will appear
and with them, the past
and with them, the end of rain
and new futures in our hands.

Everything is cracking
where light is shining
interrogating.

Again and again, we make the
journey
blind, our eyes shut
so the beautiful cannot look
on all the horror
and we can dream again
without history.

English language versions by Maria McManus

Eilish Fisher

Eilish Fisher grew up in rural Vermont and moved to Ireland in 1998. Her poetry has been published in various magazines and literary journals and she was awarded third prize in the 2018 Bray Literary Festival Poetry Competition and shortlisted for the same prize in 2017. Her first children's novel was shortlisted for the 2018 Mslexia Children's Novel Award. She was awarded a Doctorate in Medieval English Literature from NUI Maynooth.

Candle-making at Winter Solstice

The table now covered in newspaper and tin
stands a solemn altar, leaning towards sink and hob.

She boils the wax in a coffee can scrubbed clean,
silver as a star. Beeswax bubbles egg yolk rich.

She moves tin to table, stretching wicks straight
before gentling them into smaller hands.

The songs are honey from the beams
dripping candle-slow as one by careful one

the children revolve to dip, smooth, dip again.
They watch the form thicken, songs heighten.

The deep scent will follow them through time
as year upon year they remember in far reaches

the light from a single flame calling them home.

Ewa Fornal

Ewa Fornal is a visual artist. She moved to Dublin in 2009 and has exhibited in group exhibitions in Ireland and abroad. A short story featured in *Crannóg* magazine. Her visual work has been published in *Chaleur* and *Theory* magazine and has also appeared on personal blogs and websites. As a foreigner living in Ireland she explores the process of writing in a second language.

Poland

Poland, will you give me a kiss?
I have no place to throw up
Your whitewashed lies
Hang on the line
Called a country flag

A chain of men in black dress
– fat parasites –
You have invited them to the table
So *the Other* was asked
To leave

You laughed: *'Hitler did the job for us*
getting rid of the Other'
Though he went further and got rid of YOU

A white eagle on red blood
Protects a nation with blue eyes
From *the Other*

Who's *the Other?*

A Black?
A Jew?
A Homo?
A Single mother?
A Disabled person?
A Refugee?

A white eagle with his legs spread apart
Like a hooligan ready to start a fight
Nationalism in my blood
Like a train inside my vein
Like a drunk passenger on Ryanair
I have to hold myself back
From throwing the grenade of
WHO I'VE BEEN MADE TO BE
I have to work hard
To recognize
WHO I WANT TO BE

They don't understand me
Because there is no ME

I am *the Other*
To the country I come from
And I'm *the Other* to the country I've come to
I'm *the Other* to my mother and to my father
I'm *the Other* to you
And to myself

I'm on Neither-land
I'm on Neither side
Of the fence
Because I'm wrong if I go to the left

43

And I'm wrong if I go to the right
My *belong* is nowhere to be found

I haven't yet made it to land

Or I can sway from side to side
With my drunken steps
I've left something behind
And I haven't yet reached
What's ahead of me

Is there anything ahead?

Nicola Geddes

Originally from Scotland, Nicola Geddes studied at the Glasgow School of Art, and the London School of Music. Based in County Galway for the past twenty five years, she works as a cellist and tutor. Her publication credits include: *The Irish Times, Crannóg, The Galway Review, Crossways, The Blue Nib, Skylight 47* and *Poethead*. Awards include: Special Commendation, Patrick Kavanagh Award 2017; Highly Commended, 2018, The Over the Edge New Writer of the Year. In May 2019 she won the *Irish Times'* New Irish Writing Award.

After September

These are the lonely days of the far shore
A restless ocean staggers and churns
between me and all my grieving kin
Cries lost in the ruthless gale
These are the salt-sting days of remembering

Shelter me on the island
Gather me in soft lilac wool
Fill my hands with painted eggs
Remind me of the tender days
before loss crashed through the glass
and flooded all our stories.

Kitchen

I dream of a home.

I tell this to the walls in the kitchen
of my rented house
Although they look strong
I cannot trust them
I need walls that will not crumble
Walls that can withstand a phone call
a letter, or a knock on the door

In another dream, I give it all away
I feel light, filled with bravado
But in the kitchen, the feeling ebbs
I think of my pots and pans
and of my silver ladle

In a different time
I would be buried with my soup pot
shining at my feet
My cold ladle clasped
in my cold hands folded
over my still heart
All my children
and all their children
would remember me
warmly

But that's another fantasy
In this life I have but one child
and she is nearly grown

I lay my hands on the old wooden table
on its way to be couped a decade ago

but resurrected
held together by the stains of turmeric and beetroot
by fidgets of candle wax
by the sounds of a girl practising her guitar
by the pages of sheet music she leaves there daily
by the faint shimmer of jumbled letters
that transfer through her homework notes
onto the soft pine surface

In a matter of months the girl will be gone.
Table, what will hold us together then?

Native

> *'Here's the bird that never flew, here's the tree that never grew*
> *Here's the bell that never rang, here's the fish that never swam'*
> *– Verse associated with Glasgow Coat of Arms*

I flew far from that city
towards a town that thought itself a city
towards a September that smelled of turf
and a bell that rang, at six o'clock every evening

I swam an ocean and a sea
to find an island in the palm of my hand
The rain tasted of salt
Gentians and purple orchids
sprang from cold grey stone
Summer brought visitors and bicycles
and autumn passed without leaves
into the gales and quiet of winter
until the gentians again

After five turns of that gold ring
I sailed back across the bay
carrying much more
my pockets full of pebbles
I followed the river and the stone walls
They brought me on the salmon's journey

After twenty more turns of that gold ring
(see how it goes faster now)
I saw that I am the tree that grew away from its roots
but I grew on, reaching into the peaty soil by the castle
I left some roots in the hedgerows
under sloes, hawthorn, and vetch
I left some in the cracks of limestone shelves
and in the forestry track under the tread of dogs' paws
Perhaps I already left roots here –
they will survive if they get past the concrete

All this turning and returning
has left me uncertain
of the way home.

Skin

Is my skin the boundary of me?

I asked the great gull
the whitest egret
and the ancient heron

but what do my feathered selves
care for boundaries?

I asked the silver mackerel
reflected in the highest clouds
I asked the shell
of the sideways little crab

but all that was there
was air

I asked inland
down in the small corners
where skin is covered
in grey-brown fur
all the way up
to bright black eyes
listening

my ears prickle
listen, mouse whispers
there is no other

our bird self
could be that circling hawk.

Sound Sleep

a childhood between two pianos

A school night; homework done
Mum in the front room
her freckled arms glide above the keys
her fingers dance Preludes and Fugues

Follow me through the kitchen
Bach will recede but the centuries are fluid
We can time travel by just walking through the house
The future approaches as we brush our teeth

Next to our bedroom the sculptor of sound
in his egg-box lined garage
turns motifs around in his hands
plays with colour, finding keys to other worlds

Snug in our bunks, we are lulled
by the harmonies of the next century
Certain of our place in this story
we glide through galaxies in our sleep.

Voyager

The centre of our solar system, you
placed a yellow football on the kitchen linoleum.
Craig, being older, and being Craig, knew
the order of the planets – Play-Doh Mercury first-
yes, but Venus will need to be
and you showed him the tile
half way down the hall.
It was my job, you said
to hold onto the Earth
– a beautiful, iridescent blue marble,
at once both dark and light –
and to place it, carefully
by the garden gate

We followed you, as you followed what was to be
Voyager's path
it'll send back pictures and sounds
a red marble Mars out in the back lane, then
the delightfully messy *papier-mâché* Giants
Jupiter, whose smudged red spot stained my fingers
Saturn, pinned by its rings to an unsuspecting door

We voyaged further, to the outer reaches
Uranus brought us to Great Western Road
Neptune by the chip shop, and, only once we had walked
all the way up to the school
did you pull the dried pea from your pocket
and declare it Pluto

It'll keep talking to us, teaching us
we heard you, we received all those riches
for another forty years until
you departed the known worlds
and my hold on the Earth shifted

Now we listen for
interstellar whispers
in memory, in silence
in the inner space you left behind
in the knowledge that beyond knowledge
Voyager travels on

Charleen Hurtubise

Charleen Hurtubise is a Dublin-based writer originally from Michigan. Her poetry and other writings have appeared in various journals. Recently her poem featured in the *Hungering* curation on the Poetry Jukebox installation at EPIC Museum in Dublin. She was a participant on the Irish Writers Centre *XBorders* project. Her work focuses on identity, dislocation and the way in which unresolved trauma maps onto future generations.

The Burren

He doesn't talk to me anymore
unless it's about children or chores.
He is quiet, like his father.
I didn't know until it was too late:
there is a silence so deep it rests
like water at the bottom of a lake
crushing out all light.

It hasn't occurred to him how unhappy I am.
I walk along the cliffs, passing wildflowers that are rare.
They've found their way to this part of the world, too.
Blown here on the wind,
they take root in the crags of limestone
for a few short weeks.
And then they die.

TORNADO SIREN i hear Kansas gets them more than here but this is no comfort when the air turns a
green hue and becomes still as still as the moment a child teeters inside the second story
window of a house screen pushing further and further out   the clock will not stop
the ground will not wait he will not deliver to her arms   safety   is this how
she feels every time the whistle blows on the fire station down the
street? hot summer days that turn into violent nights?
thunder pounding all around beating rhythms to
which she moves collecting children pillows
matches rosaries; strong Arms gathering
out of sleep dragging us down
to the basement for safe-keeping?
gathered on the cool,
cement floor chanting
Hail Marys with our eyes
closed tight
dryness gathers in the
corners of our mouths
kix cereal spider eggs
clinging to our fingers
lightning strikes
closer and closer
floorboards creak
stay still, stay quiet
she warns
under fear of breath
moving towards us
in the distance
is the
whistle
of a train
is the turn
of a lock
is the
hinge
on a
door
is
Our
Father's
heavy
boots
upon
the
s
t
a
i
r
s

53

Chris Jones

Chris Jones was born in New York and grew up in Co Kerry. He has a BA in Fine Art and is also a photographer. His poems look inward at his own experience, loss and remembering, but also at his place in the world post marriage referendum. He is married to a Catalan man and lives and works in Dublin.

Hands

Your hands built this house,
bone to brick, a roof and 5 beds
between fields of cows and silage,
hands that brought pipes of water
across the field from the well,
which froze each December
while we shivered in the kitchen
making toast on the heater.
Hands bigger than mine
crooked from engines, black deep in bogs,
the nicotine years and cleaning of pipes,
hands that clattered me,
sent me flying, sent me crying
outside the pub that one time
for robbing cigarettes to smoke in the ditch.
but held me close at football matches
between the frothy roars of towering men.
Hands that hung sheep from a tree
that day when I spied,
behind the shed, the terrored eye

and the blood
and the blood
and the blood
a freezer of mutton to feed us that winter.
Hands that held hers
while the machine pumped her chest,
up and down
up and down
up and down
till they turned it off
and we went home without her.
Hands that wore my shoulders round
the buttonhole I gave you
that day in September when I married him
and told me that you were proud,
hands that are smaller now, quieter now,
that live another life, hands that I see in mine
lines etched, like spiders across milk,
running from time.

The Green Buddha

I dropped it, it fell
not in slow motion like in the movies,
but in a flash, crumpling in on itself like a foil wrapped egg.
Fear dashed and rose in my throat, my ears.
I was four maybe five. You cried.
Carefully gluing it, your anger a bristle.
'I'm sorry. where did you get it?'
'On a street in New York' – a whisper.
I did not know why you were crying.
After you died, it moved in with me to live on a window.
Wrapped in my luggage it came
to the searing heat of Barcelona and back again.

I imagine you as a young woman, not yet nineteen,
arriving on Manhattan Island, in the wrong shoes.
I imagine you in the John Barleycorn bar, on East 45th Street,
eating the best cheese burger in the city, pretending to be twenty-one.
In my fortieth year I go back to where I was born.
Under the clatter of elevated trains, I walk through Jackson Heights,
nostalgia for a place that I can't remember,
Queens, with a house at the end of a street.
I imagine you, hair long to your waist,
straightened smooth with an iron and brown paper
on a beach on Coney Island.
I imagine you writing letters to your mother,
blue airmail envelopes sending money back home.
In a photo, you are standing with your head thrown back,
laughing by a pool, brown and lean as a greyhound.
Before our father, before all of us,
I imagine you some faded summer
between plumes of steaming manholes and jigsaw fire escapes.
I imagine you on a street somewhere in New York City,
a cigarette against the winter sky, hurrying home
with your green Buddha.

Kayssie Kandiwa

Christie 'Kayssie' Kandiwa is a 21-year-old business marketing student and copywriter, with a passion for poetry and music. She was born in Zimbabwe and grew up in Ireland. Her works strive to blend themes of Zimbabwean culture with her Irish upbringing. Her writing may be found in the magazines *Seventh Wave* and *Unapologetic*. She aims 'to promote mental-health and equality in all its forms with themes of reflection, self-identity and resilience.'

Mwana WeZuva *(The Child of the Sun)*

Her bodice
Readily burnt
Glowing within the ashes,
Markings of whips, lashes;
Bodily garnishes –
Vilifying her levigated bones to be used regardless.
Her eyes ablaze,
A burning furnace
Cremating her bones.

> *'I'll be flexible now –*
> *I'll fit where I don't belong now –*
> *No need to pretend to be weak now –'*

My skin is crude oil,
Submerging these titanium bones. Holding a temple of jewels
More expensive than the black diamonds in my eyes –
The slave swallowed me through her eyes –

And I swam to her belly –
Where I was reborn.

Mwana WeVhu *(The Child of the Earth)*

This soil is my own –
Red like the blood of my ancestors,
And orange like the tongues of fire.
Moulded from full fists of earth and rocks,
I have now become the minutiae of my visage.

I am the terracotta of the gods,
Broken and burnt,
Ground into dust like a brown-sugared virago.

I've come to realise that –
These winds not only bear the whispers of the trees
But the secrets of the spirits
That let my past slip away
Between the fingers of Éire.

I have rooted myself here long enough,
I now recognise them as my thoughts.
This soil is mine,
I am a skin-walker of my own lineage.

Mwana WeMvura *(The Child of the Water)*

Shivering
I've carried my hands
finger by finger to your shore –
This giving will scream the whispers of the hurt
My lips refuse to articulate.
I lay them behind your teeth –
That the washing and the backwash of your tongue
Shall find its way to them,
Swallowing them as your own –
And my verity will burn its way to your belly
And repose in its hollows with the truths,
And the half-truths and untruths clamour
Beating into the walls
Until they are regurgitated
And spilled in a thousand colours.

Mwana WaMai *(The Mother's Child)*

I was baptised in her waters,
Nowhere near her skin.

Submerged between the walls of her abdomen,
Drowned murmurs chanting my exorcism
While I squirmed in her still lakes
For a break free,

I dipped head-first in the cold waves of her existence,
And let my past slip away in her waters,
Awakening.

Nithy Kasa

Nithy Kasa is a poet from the Democratic Republic of the Congo and lives in Dublin where she is a member of the Dublin Writers' Forum since 2014. Her work first appeared in *Embers of Words,* the first migrant anthology published in 2012 by Migrant Writers and Performing Artists. Since then she has read widely and has given talks at the National University of Ireland Galway and the Royal Irish Academy on Language and Migration.

Accents

My accent lingered at bay,
bleaching its skin, hips tucked into a corset,
chewing English.
It cleansed its feet with the salty water
then sat on a boulder, talking to itself,
instructing the tongue how to pronounce,
but it would do otherwise.

'They will know you got here by boat not by bicycle.'

The days spent passing verbs through a needle's orb,
knitting phrases, the pricking made you kneel
to your toddler self.

I came to send this trouble away,
English is not mine to keep.

Benjamin Keatinge

Benjamin Keatinge is a Visiting Research Fellow at the School of English, Trinity College Dublin. From 2007 to 2016 he worked as Lecturer in English literature at South East European University, North Macedonia. His poetry has appeared in *Orbis, Eborakon, The Galway Review* and *Agenda.* He is editor of *Making Integral: Critical Essays on Richard Murphy* (Cork University Press, 2019). Based in Ireland, he travels frequently to North Macedonia, Greece and Bulgaria.

Passover

> *I had no rest in my spirit . . . but taking my leave of them, I went from thence into Macedonia.*
> — *Second Epistle to the Corinthians, 2:13*

Because my land has water
more than wine
because my griefs were sheltered
from the wind
I made to travel
to the land of honey-blood
with mountains and a desert
and a trine of Gods
a river and a vineyard
and a host of tongues
a people and a highway
and a cusp of pasts.

I climbed Mount Korab in the sun
knelt at Saint Panteleimon

the heresy was to stand still
the trick was to move on.

A Postcard from FYROM*

Here lies a country that lacks a name
held between the mountains and the sea,
I wonder whether geography's to blame.

Its climate and religions are the same
as hereabout and people here are free,
but it's a country bargaining its name.

Some people wonder how this nation came
to be, and say it isn't or it ought not be,
I wonder whether history's to blame.

Anyway, who cares? These lands are plain
or fair by any name that they agree,
and so a country lives without its name.

There's not much left for anyone to claim –
ancestral mountains or a missing sea –
I wonder is there anyone to blame.

People live here fiercely just the same
repeating – each to all – their history,
this country here requires a name
I wonder whether everyone's to blame.

> * FYROM is an acronym for the 'Former Yugoslav Republic of
> Macedonia' which was the official name of North Macedonia from
> 1993 to 2019 prior to the Prespa Agreement between Republic of
> Macedonia and Greece.

Borderland

They crossed to Europe
as borders closed
with stragglers camping
on the Kilkis side,
a new home
of dialects and names
olive groves and light,
and shadows walking
from Solun to Kostur,
sad trespassers
still walking
where Macedonia cleaves.

Shannon Kuta Kelly

Shannon Kuta Kelly was born in Lincoln, Nebraska and is a published travel writer as well as a poet. Her work has appeared in *Poetry Ireland Review*, *The Tangerine* and *The Irish Times*. In 2018, she was named one of the best new British and Irish poets of the year, and she holds a master's degree in writing from NUI Galway.

In Flight

Consider for a moment the sooty tern, who, when she jumps
for her first flight, will fly for three years continuously

The windows of commercial jets, three panels and bleed hole
the only space between oneself and the clouds, the fall

Lucifer, 'bearer of light', the bookmark between heaven and hell –
What can one make of the bleeding light around the morning
    star in a black sky?

They say the hero Lleu Lleu could not be killed during day or night,
neither indoors nor outdoors, not naked, not clothed, not
    walking, not riding

But I am more interested in the Roma I see in their donkey carts
in the midday sun, dusty fields, staring at them through our
    train windows

The lone synagogue which slept quietly in my home city, the
    high-ceiling

entrance room where we would veil our heads in jewel-tone
   scarves

When we turned 13, Mama warned that wild spirits would
   descend
upon our house and slam the cupboards, spill our hot soup

My right ear cocks itself toward the neatly-diced syllables
of the lady in An Post. My left ear cranes eastward, like a lost bird

Mama used to sing us to sleep, and I remember her songs,
recite them in foreign whispers to women near me on the
   rocking train

The womb is an apt, if overused, metaphor. I consider, instead,
   the tapestry
I bought in Gdansk that unravels itself between wool yarn and
   blanket

The blank pages between Old and New Testament in this hotel's
   Holy Bible,
the abandoned bus stop in my home city where occasional
   mistaken busses

still halted by accident at times, like hauntings, like mirages. Are
   we coming
or going? Sit and share this bottle with me. Look through this
   three-pane window

at the birds in the naked trees. Consider with me, *prosze*, the
   treeline, neither fully pine
nor sky – an arrow pointed upward, taut and ready at any
   moment to spring back

and fly

Sven Kretzschmar

Sven Kretzschmar is a poet from the southwest of Germany and an alumnus of Saarland University, the University of Luxembourg and UCD. His poetry has appeared in a number of magazines and journals in Europe and overseas, and with the Belfast-based Poetry Jukebox project. He was awarded 1ˢᵗ prize in the 2018 'Creating a Buzz in Strokestown' competition. He is also the illustrator of *Grimwig* and *Bert Borrone's Perpetual Motion*.

Upon Arrival in Dublin

In this run-down place with its wide stairs
and landings I will sleep for the five fitful nights.
At this small basin I will wash, and in it will clean
my clothing and linen – I teach, research, flat-

hunt from a six-bed dormitory. One foot in the door,
the other on the streets, constantly hopping from hostels
to hotels to B&Bs and back, for the better part of three
months, at some times halfway living in a UCD cube farm.

Neither fitting in with the properly settled property
owners nor with the boozy folks at the inner-city
evening corner, with English too good for a foreigner

and not good enough to be Irish –
a philosopher trying to move on to pastures new.
A strange heart looking for home and a new beginning.

Bus to Clonee

John's fiddle in the concert hall way back still echoes
in my ear on the bus from Belfield to Clonee –
back from the office, back for the night.

A booze-shrouded construction worker next to me,
who hopped on at Ashton Quay, opens another Karpackie,
facing a masterpiece of solitude in the dark windscreen

of the upper deck on which nobody is supposed to make their stand.
We hold on to handrails and our incognito day after day
driving back to bedroom towns full of strangers

like ourselves. We buy what's broken, put cash in hand
for a place to stay, to live, ignorant of previous tenants'
dirt between floorboards we're meant to learn to call

home. In the evening sky I spot a flicker of lights following
an invisible path down somewhere, out of here,
into the distance of night. Back in the house I should make time

to write a letter to my family – another letter I won't send
telling how I spend time between a place I love
and a place that I've ended up in, if only for now.

I will write my way into this new life, one line at a time.

Suzzanna Matthews

Suzzanna Matthews has lived and studied in Latin America, Europe, and Asia. Her short fiction, essays, and poetry have appeared in various American journals and magazines. She currently lives with her partner in Donegal, where she is working on a collection of short stories inspired by her upbringing, living with her maternal Native American family, and the experiences of her paternal, second-generation Irish-American family.

Resting, at St. Stephen's Green

Hard grip on the park bench – hands pressed down,
curled around, the edge of the seat
   To keep steady

My fingers feel the rough of it, the grain of the planed timber,
They trace the transitions and shifts
   Trace – hypnotic – the toothed ridges to waxy smooth,
the patina of time scored on wood

I'm almost asleep with the wear of the week's work,
A sleep without rest,

Looking straight ahead into nothing but more of the same
Nothingness and never enough-ness

I think of the man at the market who, as if he knew,
Reached out to touch my shoulder – gentle – after I'd paid,
stuffed receipt into my pocket rough,

this worry, working three jobs not enough for Dublin life and
rent – it shows
    eyes trace the notches and folds
the patina of time marred on flesh

A man walks by the bench I sit on – walks slow, in tattered
muddied shoes
And change falls cataclysmic to the ground,
rolls over and ruins the calm of the leaf dampened walkway
    St. Stephen's Green

I bend, and ache forward my right arm,
to pick up, to help put back

Feel the grit of the ground clung on, wipe it clean off the surface
Cold, smooth — and return the coin to stained paper cup,
Held by hands that are shaking – and shake

And when I stand, it begins to rain

Teaching English, at Spencer Dock

I am on the bus home – to you
The teal and cold, gold, signs of the many Centra shops blur
through the windows,
We pass the matador–bullseye reds of the Toltecas and Tescos
    and Ladbrokes.
I look out the window at the winter mid-afternoon,

It's rainy
It's raining
It rains

These are the words – the vocabulary my students learned today
My *Saudi ladies* as you like to call them

I am on the bus home
From the docks through city centre.
Passengers board, muffled in thick coats, and it smells of damp
    dog's fur,
the rain on wool of hats and scarves
I am jostled, and feel strangers struggle to keep their breath away
    from my ears
and back of my neck

I am on my way home where you will ask,
'What happened today?'

Terrified
Terrifying
Humiliated – ashamed

These are words
I was asked to teach today

After a student broke from terse nods to tears,
Told me that teen boys, threatened and shoved
Spewed words she could not understand,
on breath hot with alcohol, directly into her face,
her with her small children on the Luas,
Told me that days before older boys tore off her daughter's hijab
As she walked home from school alone, flung it to the ground
    and stomped

This is not the first of these stories, I hear,
They are not the first of these stories I tell you,
They are different versions of the same

I know what you will say sarcastically, *Modern Ireland*
Words I've heard broadcast-touted, read in bold font headlines, then
spoken near-mournful with a shake of the head,
By the *auld* ones at your home-house in your west country village

I walk away from the flash new-tech buildings at the docks,
I walk away from my student's warm homes, fed on golden Al
    Lugaimat,
amber dried tamarinds, tasting still, the saffron of the coffee Arabic

I walk in the cold and rain to the bus
Past the reminding, plaintive bust of Luke Kelly,
Past a church fence painted rainbow colours – reading pride

But there, angry young boys go past me

Running,
Rushing,
Stumbling

As I wait for the bus home to you

Jaki McCarrick

© Bobbie Hanvey

Born and raised in London, Jaki McCarrick is an award-winning writer of plays, poetry and fiction. Her poems have been published in numerous journals and anthologies. Her most recent play, *Belfast Girls,* developed at the National Theatre Studio, London, premiered in Chicago in 2015 to much critical acclaim and has since been staged many times. Her story collection, *The Scattering* (Seren), was shortlisted for the 2014 Edge Hill Prize.

Camomile

Fair fur-headed sisters
all on one woody stem,

my mother would gather
your blonde-dye heads

from the parks of Kilburn
and Hampstead, and boil you up:

gold for her hair
and for her children's

though I was dark
as a secret.

Your bombshells
sweeten the air.

An infusion of your whole
dried body calms

the unquiet part of the heart
and worries kidney stones.

From the Greek *khamaimelon*,
meaning 'earth-apple',

your yellow melon-heads
indiscriminately perfume

battlefields
as they do suburban lawns –

and bring today
to this cluttered desk

my mother,
that platinum-haired apothecary.

Sanatogen Wine

A cane and teak mustard-coloured divan, a leathered bellows,
like a cittern. A view to the whitewashed yard and outdoor
toilet. In the front room a Chinese tea-set, still in its box,
which my sister and I raffled in a Sale of Work for local

orphans in our first week home; a cabinet filled with souvenirs –
evidence of the kind of travel even my mother had not done.
Her spinster aunt's house (and her inheritance) was dapper,
Oriental, filled with antiques, a Bakelite Radio.

Upstairs, black-rimmed silk and cotton quilts like kimonos,
wallpaper that stared me down to darkness every night:
a curvilinear pattern of blue ribbons round a small red rose.
Books: Blake, Nabokov, Goldsmith, Saki – source of my future

name. And when we first arrived, everywhere empty bottles
of Sanatogen Tonic Wine – suggesting a vice or panacea,
the yellow label a medicinal-looking cover for its 15% vol.
The house was instant history for a family that had none,

coming from London as we did. At the heart a wooden banister
that I can still feel beneath my hand, with its trace of my father's
hand, my siblings' and mother's, my great-aunt's, too –
on her way downstairs, perhaps inebriated, to her dark elaborate
    rooms.

Kathy in the Kitchen

I'm starting to remember things about the 80s:
It's raining in London, the air is pearl-grey,
there's a white glimmer off vinyl-black streets.
I've not gone to university, am spending my time

listening to Joy Division, reading Kathy Acker.
I go to see her one night at Riverside Studios.
A small shaved head, she's tall and smokes,
has poems about pornography, a Jewish mother;

the crowd is a mix of young, punk and gay.
I've not thought of this reading for two decades
then into this afternoon's routine and drudgery –
a flash of her coiled in leather like a wet street.

Home Ground

after Geoffrey Hill

It's a true border town in the wild west tradition ...
it never seems a place where you or for that matter the locals
can feel fully at ease.
— 'The Rough Guide to Ireland'

I have returned after a long absence
to a notorious border town.
No one made me come here.
My eyes were open leaving London,
the South Bank, St. Martin's Lane,
the 98 bus, the delicious gust of air
you'd get down St. John's Wood tube,
those empty imperious galleries
all along Kensington Church Street
seen best from the top deck of the 52.
I didn't think I'd miss them but I do.
When I was there I would think of here,
the salt-blown air of this unregenerate town
where alternate views of history can be found.

Midnight in Cricklewood

By the Galtymore men hunch up
on collapsing grey street-frames
as if watching market day in Carrick.

Another morning exiled,
another day of plaster and bricks
and now the trapped stink of the Broadway.

Soon the air has the scent of bagels,
the kitchens of Thailand and Ethiopia
offering lotus flowers, spices.

Here in the maw of the sleepless city,
where all the world's tribes mingle,
men build the myths of small towns.

Shoe Story

How did the ground feel, father,
in London, concrete under your feet,
after the green lanes to the house,
the deep, slow meadows to the crocus-rimmed pond?
And when you returned home in July
did the rhythm of hill-walking cradle your insteps?
Mine knew the difference and they told the earth.

The Architect

> 'I have a journey, sir, shortly to go;
> my master calls me, I must not say no.'
> — *Kent, King Lear, v., iii*

> *i.m. Michael Mehremitch*

i

Close to dusk I look for undertakers.
I find a number in the phone directory
and ask my sister if they will do.
The company is close by on a street
you knew in Cricklewood.

With your body a mustard-coloured
husk outside the white sheet
in the dark room of the flat
we've been in for days,
two men arrive, in suits,

one talkative, the other silent –
his face mottled and broken in places
like Magwitch.

The flat is tomb-quiet.
None of us have slept for days.
The smells of ointments, scented candles,
oils, sweet-odoured medicines,
sugar-coat our cocoon
while the wind-chime
on the balcony
sometimes takes us from ourselves.

The dark-suited bruisers,
by now more Pinter than Dickens,
are shown to the furthest room.

I am fixated by the body's heft:
how one would lift a crate –
or a sack of grain.
The men have a long black bag
laid out on the floor, unzipped,
and are aiming to place you inside –
when they drop you:

the bones crack, the frame distorts,
my sister runs from the room.

ii

Later, around midnight,
as my sister sleeps
her terrible tear-filled sleep,
I send off emails about your passing.

The printer suddenly kicks off
and ushers in
the remains of a document
downloaded from the Science of Mind
website the day before:
someone had suggested we get you to repeat
Ernest Holmes affirmations,
and in our desperation
to hang on to your life,
we did.

I take the pages up,
am chilled to read them.
One subject had been missing
from the previous day's printout,
but here, now, are the affirmations on it:
two, three or more
on *freedom*.

iii

Boxing Day and dinner was at yours,
in the new three-storey house in Maida Vale
in which you had practiced again your signature
red and neutrals;
the basementy light warmed the dining-room,
and somehow the conversation turned to love – and bitterly.

You said love didn't matter in relationships,
that people were well to marry without it.
This caused shockwaves between you and my sister.
She looked from you to us to the other guests
as if you'd stabbed her – and in company, too.

I argued, as I often did with you,
that you were wrong.
I wanted to defuse what my sister
was inferring from your cantankerous remarks.
I think you mentioned Ayn Rand.

Much of what you used to say
I've since come round to agreeing with;
you were, after all, much older than us.
Wiser. But not on that.
There was so much love around you, Mick.
In the end it was almost creaturish.

iv

We lined up along the pier at Carlingford.
You wanted to be scattered there.
You, half-French and half-Egyptian,
Londoner, Notting Hill-er,
wanted the last of yourself
spilled into the Irish Sea.

The day was wild and silent.
I'd developed tinnitus,
(stress-induced, the doctor said)
and was locked inside my own head
listening to an orchestra
of random buzzes and booms.

My eyes remained on the ground.
I admired the denim-blue
of dry mussel shells.

Your ash felt cold and lumpy.
I would never have thought it ash.
More like damp oats
or builders' sand.

v

It started with a fall in a hotel in Ravensdale.
The first CAT scan showed nothing.
Later: grade four, malignant.
Then the decision to operate but avoid Chemo;
this choice involved much planning.
Your brain was a building to be saved
using organic materials only:
B17, coffee enemas, selenium, followed by
Meditation, Reiki, Gerson Therapy,
the daily juicing. Yet nothing
could stop that pale fruit multiplying,
as if a melon-grower worked within you day and night.

But 'the journey' was a good one for you.
You met amazing people:
Darina, the Reiki healer,
who gave you the wooden
rosary beads from Medjugorje
that you clung to till the end
and which I now carry.

vi

Axe-wound you would call it:
that deep cut in your sallow skull,
with stitches from popular depictions
of Frankenstein's monster.

The operation left you weak,
but still discernably 'you',
nothing too visibly affected,
speech sharp and barbed as ever.

But you could no longer
imagine buildings, you said.
Could no longer dream up a maze of rooms,
see their colours and shapes speaking,
as you'd done all your adult life.
This was a blank after the incision,
and did not return (as you'd hoped),
though the tumour did.

vii

Three months after your scattering,
on New Year's Day,
I walk along Templetown and Shelling Hill.

The light is warm and white
and a happy three-legged dog
wanders the beach, ownerless.

The water is slow and winter-blue
and I sense you out there,
as far as a sea-mile, and closer,

lingering on the water's edge,
in the trapped plumes
of foam in rockpools.

And you are present, too,
in the spirituous air,
not yet gone from where you'd been scattered.

By the beach-end I pick up two mussel shells
and declare them last-trace mementoes,
like old postcards, or poems.

Raquel McKee

Raquel McKee, AKA Rainbow Ashwood Jamaican, is a Caribbean born poet living on the island of Ireland who 'offers pieces of poetry which give voice to the lesser known story – the other side of the canvas – providing a new look at the identity of Caribbean people'. She is an ACNI awardee and samples of her work can be found in *FourXFour,* Issue 28 and in the 'XBorders' issue of *The Corridor.*

Resilience

Bet dem neva mention wi resilience
Wi industrious nature an wi competence
Bet dem neva mention wi stability
Trouncin slavery inhumanity

People of African descent
Veins thick with determination and grit
Undiluted by forced migration and integration
Courage coursing through capillaries to the rhythm of cutlasses,
    whisks and whips
Superior herbal remedies a superhero's cloak
Raising them to unexpected hope

Bet dem neva mention wi resilience
Wi industrious nature an wi competence
Bet dem neva mention wi stability
Trouncin slavery inhumanity

Las Casas coulda neva imagine
Im attempt fi save one people
Woulda punish anodda –
Native gatherer-fisher Tainos, flounderin under di weight o
Di workload transferred to African chattel
An eventually to combustion engine ... driven by greed whip
    and profit tyranny

Bet dem neva mention wi resilience
Wi industrious nature an wi competence
Bet dem neva mention wi stability
Trouncin slavery inhumanity

A 'servile people'?
Labelled for surviving the yoke which ground the natives to dust?
Despised for the endurance linen-millers couldn't muster?
For metronome consistency in spite of the never-
    ending bondage
Within the cloud of indentureship – a luxury they could see but
    never touch?

Inferior?
Advanced cultures confiscated, gold-mining expertise lying
    fallow in cane field heat...
Ancestral walled cities, highways with rest houses, and fine
    buildings
Eroded by being overlooked in the colonial recount
And subscripted by chattel houses overshadowed by plantation
    great houses
University students silenced with the whip of mythic ignorance ...
Musicians divested of all instruments but their voiceless voice ...

But without a wheel ... or gunpowder ...
With language oral, not written ...
The best battle plan – live to fight another day – interpreted as servility

Bet dem neva mention wi resilience
Wi industrious nature an wi competence
Bet dem neva mention wi stability
Trouncin slavery inhumanity

Caged birds singing
While strange fruit swinging
Trauma compressed into corrugated strength
Language pidgin
While cultures bridging
Integration pearled from people-trafficked sand

Bet dem neva mention wi resilience,
Wi industrious nature an wi competence
Bet dem neva mention wi stability
Trouncin slavery inhumanity

Back bruckin wuk
Mine out sweet spiritual song
Loyalty unacknowledged
Jus hone wi character
Un remembered contribution to di industrial revolution
Despite no move toward reparation fi repeated parental
    separation
Testimony to valour, moral fibre an backbone

History book nuh sing it, so mek wi sing it pon wi own

Come mek wi mention di resilience
Di industrious nature and di competence
Come mek wi mention di stability
Trouncin slavery inhumanity

Victoria Melkovska

Victoria Melkovska is Ukrainian-born with a degree in Journalism. In Ukraine, she presented and produced radio shows; moving to Ireland 15 years ago, she worked as a newspaper columnist and a foreign correspondent for the Ukrainian National Broadcaster. A dedicated member of the New Irish Communities group in the Irish Writers Centre, she enjoys exploring different writing forms under the guidance of well-known poets and authors. Alongside a first poetry collection in English, she is working on a historical novel which won Novel Fair 2018.

Rooted

Next to the stone threshold
she buried
the shrivelled umbilical cord.

An apple sapling marked the spot –
her offspring
close to home.

A lifetime away, in spring,
I ache, tugged by that string
back
to apple blossom
at the stone threshold.

Boy in a Blue T-Shirt

Chasing a ball on a verdant pitch,
rowdy, gangly, with milk moustaches –
schoolboys shake off beads of sweat
from sunburned foreheads.
Messy cowslips, croaky voices, strong legs.
'Yay!
                    It's a goal!
                                        What a shot!'
When I ask my son who scored,
he waves his hand, points,
                    'That boy,
                                        in the blue T-shirt!'
And I search for a boy in blue,
while the team
raises up,
                    rocks,
                                hurrays its hero,
the only lad on the playing field
with black, almost purple skin;
just 'a boy in a blue T-shirt'
to my son and his soccer team.

The Back Door

* *Traditionally, Ukrainian houses have only a front door*

1.

Where I come from,
winter drowses on the window ledge,
scratching glass with bristle,

lies in wait for a slightest chance
to stick its foot in the door,
to slither inside,
twirl in for a second
and stay forever.
The leather-upholstered door
with a constellation of studs,
locked, latched,
chained like a dog,
guards
my childhood's Land of Plenty
against minus twenty.

2.

'If not for a random storm,
Irish winters are mild and warm.
Come to visit this Christmas,
Mother.'
She sighs, 'Not this year. Another.'

3.

She comes;
gapes at the weird ensemble:
grass-covered lawns,
the cherry-tree blossoms fall,
a hare under a palm tree –
all in the midst of December.
But to her
one thing
is the strangest of all.
Not my ceiling-mounted windows, no.

Not stepping on the pleasantly heated floor.
She wonders at something so trivial:
my back door.
And her fingers smelling of dill
tremble turning the key,
to let in
the thrush song,
as if winter,
left many miles away,
could catch on
and invite itself in.

4.

Back home,
I smile into a watermelon slice:
A bowl of raspberries on the ledge,
crispy apples, soft pears
just where the winter slept.
My son's honeyed kiss
lands on a pancake of his grandma's cheek.
A new back door to the garden swings
(letting in
the chirruping whirl,
the flies too,
the smell of barbecue)
and bangs behind him.

Two Letters

1.

Dear Grandad,
hope my letter finds you well
in that white-washed house
with roast pumpkin smell,
where you taught me
to count flies
in the frost-laced window.
It's been a year in a foreign land,
and now at last
I can honestly tell you
about my life in Ireland.

When I arrived in early spring,
the daffodil-scented air seemed so clean,
I swayed like a bar-fly around.
But that was before –
before I found
the tight twisted roads,
the low-rise towns,
dog shit underfoot,
chewing gum on the ground,
and broken umbrellas trembling
in a bicycle lane.

Georgian terraces look the same;
the red-brick streets just differ in name.
And what would surprise you even more,
no one takes off their shoes indoors.
(The shoes, I admit, don't get dirty).

My low-ceiling room has musty stink,
a coin meter and a personal sink.
The taps are so short as if made for kids
to wriggle, for fun, their fingers.

The people, however,
that's a different story.
Simply put,
if you step on someone's foot,
you'd hear a humble 'Sorry';
a stranger would randomly say 'hello'
and thank a bus driver
(I wonder what for).
Yesterday,
running to my English class
I stopped when I heard laughter
at a funeral mass –
the Irish come to bid farewell
often to near strangers.

Being devoted and feckless in turns,
they tuck in *black* buggies their newborns.
Mum, insulated in a scarf and worn Uggs,
her baby, in a light frilled dress, barefoot
(or just with one sock, if lucky).

And the milky knees of Irish school-girls
flash all year round,
tremble like those umbrellas,
left to the mercy of wind.

Cafes put shutters down at seven, and
if I fancy to meet with a date or a friend
I enter a pub: noisy and smelly,
with the shouts and cries

and the blaring telly.
But, dear Grandad,
you mustn't fear:
I don't drink whiskey,
I don't drink beer;
I usually order black tea with milk;
white tea, the Irish call it.
I like it.

2.

Goodness, my dear,
What nonsense you've written here!
I utterly fail
to make of your letter head or tail.
Please, fetch a pen
and write your answers:
How much is
salted herring (two ounces)?
How much money
you pay for a jar of three liters of honey?
What about other familiar goods:
ten eggs,
a bucket of rooster spuds;
a sack of sugar;
a loaf of rye bread.
I will decide
by knowing all that
whether your life in Ireland
is worth the ticket.

Rafael Mendes

Rafael Mendes was born in São Paulo, Brazil and was raised between the former and Franco da Rocha. He has lived in Ireland since 2016. His first poetry collection, *Um ensaio sobre o belo e o caos,* was published in 2018 by Editora Urutau, and his poems have appeared in magazines, journals and on RTÉ's *Poetry Programme.*

after the james larkin house shooting

a bullet hole in the wall
was filled in with cement
painted in gold
and recycled
as a goalpost

on o'connell bridge

a seagull flies over a passerby
pounces
and gives a sausage roll
wings

32 kg suitcase

before I left home
I packed a 32 kg suitcase

I still have some
of the clothes and books
shoes and photographs
my grandmother's notes and coins collection
and memories from my first ever flight

the suitcase is still here
covered in dust

if I was to come back
what would I pack?

a red brick from henrietta street
a slang dictionary from the north inner city
burdock's fish and chips
bookshops: books upstairs and chapters
fragments of stories from smokers
huddled in doorways

but how can I go back
after leaving home
I became a stateless citizen
with a 32 kg suitcase

staring at stars

searching for the ideal word
as if mumbling about sand
to find the smallest sapphire

as a needle piercing flash
a shower dripping warm fog
an ambulance howling somewhere

a word shining in the dark

dart workers

men are working on the railway tracks
what are they doing

polishing the cold rail
and settling gravel down

musicians
tuning their instruments

before the operatic note
that will tear apart

darkness
and silence

a beauty

grandmother was a beauty
in tailored clothes
           (red is the colour that wakes her in my memory)
her skin smelled of vanilla
from the body lotion that
she religiously applied every morning

grandmother was a modern woman in the 1970s
she challenged dictatorship
fired two husbands

moved to the big city
wrote her story while working through
endless sewing machines
and raising five kids

grandmother died of cancer

in her last months in hospital
she wore red
and tiny gold earrings

she smelled of cancer
and vanilla

she kept smoking

historian

I dreamed of being a historian
in that neighborhood with
      no paved streets, no internet connection
      no books, only borders, faith in god and forgetfulness

I dreamed of being a historian
among one-way conversation with action toys
laughter of alcoholic card games
mad old people collecting white stones
(one swore that someday these would be
as valuable as a black opals)

I dreamed of being a historian
in what books I could find belonging
in words I understood silence
in a place beyond nowhere

I dreamed of being a historian
of the place I came from
where we couldn't afford electricity
and streets were called summer, autumn,
winter and spring

I dreamed of being an historian
writing the history of the cloth
we used to wipe out muddy shoes
before getting the train

east wall road

white smoke
cotton in a gaseous afterlife
draws across the road
an industrial veil

on the left an antique market
no car was ever seen entering
the word goes that the owners wait
for their sons to come back

across the street a vast and roofless car park
the first B&B for brand new cars
that sailed the ocean into Ireland

an italian takeaway owned by indians
a traditional chinese medical centre
a dance studio, a radio station, a childcare
seabank house with its famous carvery lunch

then lidl with its automatic cutter
makes the experience of buying a loaf
as amusing as a slice topped with
avocados and poached eggs

reaching the end of the road
a huddle of semi-detached
each with its window

shut off to the traffic
of cars, bicycles and passersby

rooks, coal tits and swans
sharing the stream ahead
which becomes a rink
of small pleasures

são paulo

O my beloved city

your roar
>
> of helicopters landing
> on financial buildings
> shouts of traders
> blaring motorcycles
> crisscrossing the city
> always desperately late

your texture
>
> concrete and flesh
> raw materials
> for what was built
> of the town
> by immigrants from the northeast
> who own nothing of it

your warmth
>
> summer afternoons that suddenly shuttle
> from maya blue to a heavy grey
> to black blurring into rain
> sweating on trains and subway lines

your aromas
        at the town market
        fresh amazonian fish
        beside tricolour peppers
        medicinal herbs

        a step outside
        the grey smell of exhaustors and
        tietê river – our ancestor's truthful river –
        now a filthy steaming bog
        clogged with garbage

your characters
        hippies having a barbeque in front of j.p. morgan
        pastors chanting that jesus will return
        and infidels will be crushed
        kids juggling at traffic lights
        as shut-tight windows slide past

O my beloved city
        wherever I go
        I will spread your word

Juliana Menezes

Juliana Menezes is a Brazilian Portuguese language teacher, with degrees in Education and in Journalism, and is the founder of the Portuguese Language Centre in Dublin. She has been writing since a young age, mainly poems and short stories, with some of her work being published through competitions. She moved to Ireland in 2007 where, along with her poetry writing, she is currently working on her first novel in English.

Layers of Me

One day I woke up
and I was gone.
On the floor
I saw a carpet.
Through the window,
a tree I'd never seen before.
It was shaking with passion,
orange, yellow, red leaves
all over the road,
while pedestrians jumped puddles,
clasped by coats and fat scarfs.
I noticed the cold.
By my bed, a pair of fluffy slippers,
behind the door, a dressing gown waiting.
I didn't go far,
the cracking old parquet flooring
announced my steps
and there came voices towards me.

I naturally replied
in batches of sentences, words and courtesy
unknown to me.
In my wardrobe I had clothes
I would never consider.
The contacts on my phone
were all new to me.
I read the obituaries in the paper
searching for my name.
I tucked myself back into bed
To listen carefully to my recollections.
In nearly every spiky point of my memory
I saw a curve,
a dead end
where I had to turn
and shape a new track.
Whether change meant trouble
or resurrection
I refaced my needs.
I bred certainties
and restlessly
waited for my rebirth.

Shaiyon Merkel

Shaiyon Justin Merkel was born in DC and grew up nearby in Maryland. He began seriously writing after a congenital spine condition left him immobile for over a year. He is a frequent performer in the Dublin spoken word scene, and also an avid writer of fantasy and science fiction.

My Tagore Song

Shudder the slow driven pile of mountains
where, below, cities crawl like spiders across the plain.
And unborn children cry, 'motherland, oh mother dear,
speak to me what it means to be born belonging here'.
A higher mother comes to anoint soft oils of life to their lids.
They gasp the air, they open eyes,
and find all questions answered.
They weave into the grey threads of the city
and the subtle stitching of the high mountains.
How easy it is to be born here,
how difficult to belong come death!

The ocean shills between the orange of day
and the green shadow of the monsoon nights.
Ocean's green carries inland with the sweep of rain,
painting the earth in shades of mangrove trees and rice fields.
The stitching turns to knotted forms, and still, all flows like water.
How life flows on, as though it were water!
How stories spin the weft to its weave!
Let words shimmer and flow.

Let thoughts trickle from the tongue,
in a language of sounds with no meaning,
vested in the blood but not the tongue,
and patterns for only the eyes not the ears.

Motherhood, Motherland, and the children of Mothers.
Between them, who am I?
Flower lips on soil skin; 'This is from *bɛŋ 'gɔːl*'.
All colours of the land weave together.
Like the craft of cotton fabric. The land *is* cotton fabric.
A shari which my Mashi wears,
and which I play my fingers along. I imagine the distant soil
as she tells me of Kolkata and Howrah,
Darjeeling and Siliguri, the Sundarbans and the Ganga.
And I see through her eyes
the homeland where I have never been.

Holi

Please tell the vested revellers
who wait to caper the cultural dance
that I don't celebrate Holi with paints.
I am Bangla.

But I will walk with you through Ireland
across the emerald earth which, yearning, calls,
broken into all so many voices,
and sucked through those once-*Catholic* halls.

All this, for Ireland, I will do.
I am all the same as you.

I shall set aside my Kali for one night,
and cry – *Hare Vishnu, Hare Éire.*

'Tantra'

Cha-stained teeth (in a brown mouth)
shine like white picket fences when you brush them.

White-tooth kisses, I'm willing, but that's it for him;
Brown boys vanish into brown dreams if you rush them.

Brown boys turn into white dreams when you bed them.
'Have you heard of Tantra?' white boy whispers, as the lights
    grow dim.
Brown men turn into yards with white picket fences when you
    wed them.

Nita Mishra

Dr. Nita Mishra completed her doctoral studies at University College Cork (2018), and is currently a researcher on Social Inclusion in Vietnam at UCC. She studied, worked, married and had children in India. She has also lived in Tokyo, Taipei and Bangkok. She came to Dublin in 2007 on a spousal visa, and is 'stuck' here for now with an Irish passport.

I Miss

The madness, the smell of earth, the sweat,
I miss
the crowds, the noise, the colours, and
the nip in the Delhi winter air

I miss the street savouries,
I miss shopping on Janpath, Dilli Haat, Lajpat Nagar,
the old brand Darzi
I missed out on the moment when Ritu Kumar
ceased to churn out those budget-friendly
embroidered Kashmiri Kurtis

I miss walking at Parry's Corner in Madras
running my fingers through myriad coloured beads,
exquisite laces, beautiful cotton
a treat to my eyes shopping for return gifts
for my little girl then
all the fun
which my son never had growing up
here in those initial years

I miss lessons in parenting
at the slides, the see-saws, and the sandpits
in parks bound by the four walls of housing compounds
on open beaches

I miss sitting on my rocking chair for innumerable teas
reading the TOI, constantly badgering
the 'maids', but now
I miss not being able to cook, clean or wash anything!

I miss being able to ring doorbells,
without making phone-calls,
of friends and cousins
relatives, siblings and parents
I miss introducing my children to everyone I know
or once knew
I miss taking them to places I went
growing up
I miss giving them a 'point of reference'
a history, a culture, cousins
a narrative

But all in all
I miss being
Who I thought I was!

Yameema Mitha

Yameema Mitha is from Lahore, Pakistan. Her family originally comes from Kolkata and Bombay. With a family deeply committed to education and the arts all over the Indian subcontinent, she is a devotee of Hindustani classical music. She has studied, lived and worked in Pakistan, as an activist and an educator. She met her Irish husband while studying at Sussex University, and now lives between Ireland and Pakistan.

from **A Pakistani Immigrant in Ireland**

I do not belong here
You do not need to call me names
Tell me to go home
Pick out my different colour
In your sea of paler ones
I know
I do not belong
My friends tell me vociferously
That I do
That I belong wherever I choose
They talk of no barriers and no borders
Of immigrants and migrants and rights …

In a harsh and selfish world
I am grateful for their kindness
More grateful than I should be
But kindness is hard to find
And must be treasured
So I will be grateful

Grateful for safety
Grateful that those I love
Can live unafraid
Grateful for the gracious green
Of this familiar city, this beautiful country

But I know I do not belong here
No barrier and no border
And no kindness and no comfort will cut me off
From the knowledge that the earth of which I am made
Was once the specks of dust that danced
In the light of the sun
Where the Sindhu flows ...

My body made from those motes of dust
given soul by the longing of the sound around me
The sound of music on a landscape of silence
The sounds of our gods
I call each one by name
Kharaj and Pancham and Gandhar
Rishab, Madhyam, Dhevat and Nishad ...
Woven languorously in the heartbeat of rhythm
The sound of longing
The sound of the land of my home ...

I need no names and no nations
To tell me who I am

Bruno Morando

Bruno Morando was born in Vicenza, Italy in 1991. Having completed his Masters in Economics at the University of Bologna, he moved to Dublin in 2015 to continue his studies and he is currently in the final year of a PhD in Development Economics at Trinity College. Bruno has a great passion for literature and has recently started to write poems and short stories in Italian and English.

In Smithfield

Free from bigotry and shame
Father Gilligan's flock go for brunch
Every Sunday morning in Smithfield
Happy gentrified faces
Covered in fake tan concealing
Tender white complexions
And freckles
One could fall in love with.
Armed with yoga mats
They go and find their own peace
They all smile at me
As they claim that
After all
Dublin's weather is not
As bad as people say.
I nearly cheer
As a rough voice shouts at me
To bring my focking arse
Back home.

Elizabeth Murtough

Originally from California, Elizabeth Murtough is a graduate of the MPhil in Creative Writing at Trinity College Dublin. In 2018, she was selected for the Poetry Ireland Introduction Series. Her poems have appeared in several magazines and anthologies. She is the co-editor of *Channel*, an Irish environmental magazine of poetry, prose and criticism.

Some Harvest

I am given a machete to harvest nopales.
Soon: aguacate, maíz, agave.

In the kitchen I pick thorn from flesh.
Chop, boil, toss with onion, limón, cilantro.

'Our people gave you papas,' he says into
his spoon. Papas, which drove us out

of Ireland, here. 'Ha-ha!' he laughs, a rattle like
the Hopi corn we lately rubbished,

kernels turned a home for weevils, husky
in our hands, only good for goats

and chickens. Cleaning up the kitchen – scrap
to bin and earth again – he hums: 'yesterday …

all my troubles seemed so …' far away, and returned
to the place I blood from, my hands hover

over apples I don't know the names of.
There's a different density to these

potatoes. I wouldn't call them papas.
I call to tell him so, and he says 'ha-ha!'

I can't tell – am I cold or hungry here? It's summer,
but the sun is lemon-coloured, not yolky,

like the one I come from. 'I miss
home,' I say, and hear: 'what's

home?' so I scrape my plate and lick
these tiny spoons, hum my questions holey

as a weevil given somewhere.

Animal Dreams

As I keep saying, I'm living
in a cold place now.
There are bugs I don't know,

clouds I can't reckon.
What matter though,
if I don't know

what name to give a flower?
Or if I ache
for the olive branch,

burn for the sage?
Such small dramas,
these animal dreams.

So, what?
I covet the sun.

So does the neighbour's cat,
so does the songbird,
so, too, does the grass.

Southwest Circles

When you move again,
alone to the old coast
you will learn:

>that in May the rain
>makes everything smell
>like hot cows;

that nothing is more beautiful
or more bothersome
than an Irish sun;

>that a cigarette shared with women
>on a back porch in June
>can ash out any ache;

that a house full of books,
covered in crows,
can be a church.

All of this you will learn.
You will write it down,
and press the book of it

to your chest,
where you will touch it
once a day, smiling.

> Then, a guest will call.
> He will sit himself at the table
> where you have sat

so often
eating porridge,
writing poems …

and the light will touch his shoulder
and the edges of his face
with the reverence of moths

> as he pours the wine,
> shadow colouring
> the saltshaker,

> the colander,
> the places
> your hands know …

> And when he tips
> the bottle – empty
> in the belly of your glass,

your heart will break
because you will have learned,
together, with all the corners

and the cupboards of your sweet home,
that enough is only enough
until there is more.

Emma Must

Emma Must was born in England and lives in Belfast. Her debut poetry pamphlet, *Notes on the Use of the Austrian Scythe* (2015) won the Templar Portfolio Award. Her poems are included in both *New Poets from the North of Ireland* (2016) and *The Best New British and Irish Poets 2017*. She is the recipient of an Arts Council of Northern Ireland ACES award (2018/2019).

After Ophelia

It is a Monday night in mid-October in the middle of my life
& there are trees down across Belfast & my bin has blown over
& sent the concrete block on top of it flying through the air
& the lads over the back fence are celebrating the fact
that we still have electricity by hosting a very loud disco
complete with multi-coloured flashing lights & so I am standing
outside on my back deck in my white plastic clogs slipping
on algae & patting my holly tree & looking up
at white clouds racing across the sky in the post-hurricane winds
when Reach for the Stars comes over the fence till someone shouts
to put something else on & then the night is full of Polar
(Ripperton Remix) by Vök & there is nothing to be done but
join in.

Cycling to IKEA

I went for curtains.
Beige, I thought. Linen.
I would carry them home
in my handlebar basket.

But as I pedalled along Airport Road
what unfolded
in front of me was
the fabric of a city's hem:

great warehouses and hangars,
Phoenix Natural Gas,
bird hides numbered 1 and 2,
an improbable hairdressing enterprise.

And beyond the Abercorn Basin
the cool white limbs
of a wind farm being born
or the pipes of a giant organ

transplanted from the Ulster Hall
blown out of all proportion
or a grove of silver flutes
silently fingering airs.

/ ...

I put these treasures in my basket
and in the gaps between them stuffed
storage boxes, Tupperware,
a small blue lampshade, meatballs.

Cycling back at dusk
past that hairdressers (*Hairport*,
I thought, they missed a trick)
I also acquired:

black ticks of birds
like affirmations
alighting on the surface
of the Lough, then taking off;

kids in uniform
their headphones
echoing the gantries
at Harland and Wolff;

the sunset streaming
tangerine and pomegranate
caught for a handful of minutes
in the window glass of Citibank.

Chandrika Narayanan-Mohan

Chandrika Narayanan-Mohan is a Dublin-based arts manager and writer from India, who has also lived in North America, Sweden, Turkey and the UK. She has been featured on *The Moth* and *Mortified* podcasts, with work aired on NPR and Irish radio, and regularly performs her poetry at literary and cabaret events in Dublin. In 2018 she was a participant in the Irish Writers Centre's 'XBorders: Accord' programme.

Brexit Blues

He never really leaves you.
I cry in my bathrobe, I make a playlist:
'England I love you, but you're bringing me down.'
My boyfriend is confused.
'The UK just dumped me.'
He doesn't get it.
The country leaves my veins.

I fall in love again.
I fall for an accent that fits my face,
With Dublin Bikes and 20 minute walks;
With a determined river,
With bridges and lampposts.
I think about it, I work till I burn,
And go, I'd like to make you mine forever.

But he never really leaves you,
And four years later my heart is shredded anew
I sit scared and anxious, I live on a parallel street

It's not your home anymore
It's not home, it's not home.

Would I have the courage
To defeat a faceful of spit on a crowded street?
A slur like a cut across the eyeball?
Would I be brave, would I intervene?
Would I stop him, the darkness in him?
Would I be able to stand?

Out of control, he's lashing out,
Through centuries of sickness, he was set alight
And the ugliness is a shout behind a triumphant sneer
Into the ear of terrified stranger.

I thought I felt nothing,
but it's bubbling black and viscous
As I breathe relief on Irish soil
With my heart clenched like a fist.

The 10.35 from Belfast Central to Dublin Connolly

A behemoth sweeps by in a screech of city-dust metal,
Warm blood on a cold spoon,
Dublin wintersmell.

A horror-movie clink of chains
Is only the bulk of a man
Releasing his two-wheel steed
From a pole down the middle
Of O'Connell Street.

I go North, for the night,

To speed around a different country
With voices like marbles
In pink flesh spit mouths.

It's already morning
And I return to the South,
In purple seats full of birdcage chatter.
Someone mentions Theresa May
And I can almost taste the soft melt of Cadbury's
As I decline when she offers a piece.

My phone has yet to alert me to
A change of provider and
The landscape betrays nothing:
Only graveyards
Silk-misted farmhouses
And double-glazed windows sunk into brick,
Warming in the morning sun.

Plane / Train

Legging it off the plane to be the first in line.
Striding through the airport.
Queuing for hours, itchy feet until
Bland-faced official looks,
Types,
Doesn't smile
Stamps.
Anxiety subsides.

But today I am kissing the earth with speed
Velvet hills whipping past in poison green
And bruised-lip blues.

And the only signs of crossing
Is a text on my screen.

But my face gives away what my birth right lacks
So I keep hold of my passport
As we slip down the tracks,
Just in case the wind changes direction.

The Train to Dún Laoghaire

At Salthill and Monkstown
I stare out at naked hipbones of sand, sleek in the shallow water
That deepens by the time we hit Seapoint,
Where I walked in once, delighted and numb,
Freezing the anxiety out of me
Eye-to-eye with the horizon.

But when I see that
Curve of green snaking upwards,
I remember it in darkness
Anaemic with yellow lamplight.

And I remember meeting him first, in his too-tight suit
And through the stony walls, in to meet your people,
And even in daylight, in the brightness of summer
My stomach still clenches with the memory
That I have cut you out of
So you are nothing more than a shape
At your own mother's wake.

You City, You Boyfriend

Seated awkwardly on a wooden box
We're on the last of my cigarettes, my 5th in two hours.
He talks, and talks,
(and talks)
And my replies are only punctuation for his next sentence.

Across from a grey slab tower, the city smirks,
Raises an eyebrow as if to say
'You know I'm so much better than him.'

And you're right,
Because when we converse, through the choke of soft air,
We exhale each other in whispers on a walk home
Where a smile has broken my face from the realisation that
Yes, you are better than him.

You are better than all of them, because
You push up through my thin soles and I feel every pebble
When I'm treading across your tar-bump skin
And I feel embedded in you,
You city, you boyfriend, you dusty hug.
And when I tell you that you're beautiful, you blush across the
    canal
Even though you already know that grey glamour suits you
And you don't need to be told.

I wear you like an arm across my shoulder,
And when the wind pushes my hair back
I don't need an errant hand across a café table to push it aside.
Like me, you play your cards close to your chest
But when we mourn we crack
With rain that pummels onto the pavements
And across a million cheap umbrellas.

So take me in and make me yours
Because I've already let the pollen in my pores anoint me
To an orchestra of rustling leaves and seagull song,
And one day I will take thee to be my lawful wedded home
And I shall wear a dress of summer fog
And a ring of past lives
And you will smile, and shrug,
And in your humid indifference I will vow to love you anyway
Because I'm a hopeless romantic,
And you're a city that keeps its own name.

Giuliano Nistri

Giuliano Nistri was born and raised in Rome to English and Italian parents. A science lyceum graduate, he went on to study music. After serving as an officer in the paratroops, and a period of travelling, he moved permanently to Ireland. In 2013 he published his first album of songs. He is also a freelance interpreter/translator. He writes and performs in Dublin and is currently working on his first collection of poems.

Your native home

You asked me once,
'Where does the wind go?'
I will tell you now.

After it gathers the murmuring sails
Of all the boats in the sea and tugs them to harbour
And lifts every coloured kite in the field,

After it herds the wayward clouds
Back into the sky-pen and spreads the softened pollen
Over the crust of this earth,

After it delivers each longing seed
To its solitary furrow and whistles down
The flute of resting chimneys,

After it mills the wheat in the long-shadowed farmlands
And stretches out to clink the chimes
That hang by a thread on summer porches,

After it swivels the iron-cast weathervanes to caw
Like roosters and sweeps the camphorous leaves
Into the wet ditch,

After it combs the morning fields
And braids the crowns
Of darkening forests,

After it dries yesterday's clothes on your line
And nuzzles around the working nose
Of your sleeping dog,

It finally goes home, where you came from,
And carries your father and mother
To their long-awaited sleep.

Kythira

Take me to the island
On a dinghy made of clay.

If we swung the rowlocks together,
Volleying decisive arcs into foam,
Our oars will be slings, raised
To lynch the pearled nape of the sea.

And with the keel a-flush
And a hollowing cargo hold,
Bridging the waves from brim to brim
Like a silence by one's side
Or a theft unseen,
For certain we will arrive.

Over time, the lemon trees will heighten
And terracotta jars will heap,

And the eye, trained a moment earlier upon a page
Or upon a ribbon tool, will glide down the gully
To gaze occasionally at this boat,
Bleaching in the reeds.

We will arrive for certain,
We will arrive, with a dog,
Perhaps with a son too.

It will matter little if with a missing eye
Surrendered to the sun or a hand ingrained
In the workings or if at the last minute

Happiness, like rainfall over a half-travelled sea,
Imbues everything in kind,
The expanse ahead
Like the one behind.

Rented

The off-white eviction notice writhed
Noiselessly in my cubbyhole, coiled
Around two decades of let,
Stemming time; tight tenure tourniquet.

A home dies in one's own mind first,
One's not gone yet that it vacates the breast
As if, ashamed, foreseeing the baring views,
Strips itself off walls and ceilings,

And floors. Thereon my own life's locks
Are changed and shutters fall within. Seems,
Light, which daily pooled and ebbed
In saffron hours, infusing my yard

Now struggles to flow through. The outward
Bricks are thinning, shorn by the sound
Of the street leaning increasingly
In. This dying thing that once was my

Abode will also fold to a memory
And tuck alongside those it used to keep. Dry
Weather has me stalling at the door
Regarding the blue park as ever

I did, before the ritual paper
Cast out soul from shell. I linger,
Bundled and stray like undelivered post
Then walk, among the other ghosts, a ghost.

Lianne O'Hara

Lianne O'Hara is a poet and writer from Amsterdam. She lives in Dublin, where she recently graduated from the MA Creative Writing at UCD. Her work has been published in *Writer's Block, Black Bough Poetry, Crossways* and *Amsterdam Quarterly;* her poetry was longlisted for the 2019 Palette Poetry Prize. She is currently working on a novel about experiences in prison.

Bench

cold steel son of a –

    hardwood. hard

      wood

    paint splinters

invitingly if you've

    no business

        here

stone of yesterday now

    iron pressed

into tired backs   leave

gaps almost wide enough you'd

    sink into

      sleep

roll over two cold
        shoulders trace
patterns of white bird

        leftovers
                on torn coats
future brides cast   out
this bench harbours
        much but never
                home.

Art Ó Súilleabháin

Art Ó Súilleabháin was brought up in Boston and moved to Corr na Móna, Co. Galway with his parents who always planned to return to the US. He has worked in Dublin, Castlebar and Washington DC before returning to Corr na Móna. He recently won North West Words and he has been featured in *Boyne Berries, Skylight 47* and *The Winchester Poetry Collection.* He has also published a number of books for children and regularly contributes to *Sunday Miscellany* in English and Irish.

The Soldier's Rock

It is there on the Dooras shore, not far from Cluain Bruin
nondescript, unknowable now, impossible to pinpoint.
They knew once but would not tell, Dad only half showed
it to me, pointed it out in a force five, when rolling waves
rocked the boat. I made an inexact note as we passed by,
thinking that someday I would return and try a detector
over the area, search for some relic of his presence in the
shallow earth. He was a soldier from the Armada that had
made his way inland from the storms of a western Atlantic
that swallowed dreams of conquering another foreign land
through our back door. He was buried in a grave that told
no truth about his existence, no story of his strange demise.
We learned to speak a version of English, instead of Spanish,
almost lost our own sweet tongue, rushing to adopt a stranger.

Black Love

for Polly Deacon

She was faulted for being different
in the twentieth century
a dear dear grandmother
a 'black' Protestant
from Quaker stock
falling for

a talented carpenter from the village.
He repaired furniture in winter,
gillied fishermen all summer,
she fixed the beds
at Ashford Castle.

They did not wonder at the liaison
though it may have caused talk
when John broke a previous tie
to local Catholic girl Maisie
in favour of Polly Deacon.

A priest came with a blackthorn stick
symbol of his dark authority
beat them out of the village
warned them not to return
until she had turned
and swore
that children
who might ensue
would be brought up
as pure and faithful followers.

She came back, but when her grandchild
was told that sins blackened the soul
wondered what venial or mortal meant
she told me clearly
that I should just be a 'good' boy
that 'there is no such thing as sin'.

Viorel Ploeşteanu

Viorel Ploeşteanu was born in Romania in 1972, but since 2010 has lived in Dublin. He is a graduate of the Faculty of History in Bucharest. He writes poetry, prose and theater, and has been published in numerous Romanian-language literary magazines, in Romania and abroad. He has published three volumes of poetry and six of prose. He is the founder of the magazine *Itaca*, a publication for Romanian writers abroad.

snowing in Dublin

it's snowing in Dublin
it's white and absurd
the snowfall
within us
so overwhelming
as cold silence
the emptiness in our homes
a Christmas tree
lying to us. humming
the white carols
gathering up in white
Dublin is silent
but who cares
that down in the street
another homeless man is dying
the city is cold
the lights go off

there is no one left in any of the houses
the snow is falling in vain

translated from Romanian by Daniela Elena Radu

your thought

you were nestling like a bird
beside my heart
and during this time
pieces of sunlight were falling down from the sky
as if dripping from a candle
lit for the dead;
the tears could not fall,
the keepers of sadness
with sponges in both hands
would not allow
any of the thoughts
to turn into tears;
far from all this
your thought sizzled
in my blood
like a fish
in a hot pan

translated from Romanian by Daniela Elena Radu

collect call

a little girl
upset with the crèche

or with the teacher too old
was playing outside the house
and was talking on the toy phone
with god
kind of giving out to him
or maybe not really getting along
because she told him
a bit upset
pass my mother on
she surely knows
and you'd better figure out
why in this big world
there is not one story
good enough for a girl so small

translated from Romanian by Daniela Jurj

Theia Presadă

Theia (Theodora) Presadă is a 46-year old writer from Constanţa, Romania. Since 2001 she has lived in Ireland, a country she calls 'My World, My Universe, My Future'. She has published eight volumes of poems in her native Romanian, receiving for the most recent the Award for Excellence at Vrancea literară, International Festival of Creation in October 2018. She is widely published in magazines and anthologies, and regularly illustrates or explores her writing with oil or acrylic paintings.

To all my friends from Sunday Market

Balbriggan, Co. Dublin

We all smile but I prefer the sad people
their move is terrestrial, they're rational
I resemble the dreary crowd
as only they carry the vestige of my piety
on their foreheads, on their lips,
on the dishevelled grey of their temples
I start my inner journey
I touch my every cell
my wrinkles have the clearest voice
as I'm wearing the crowd's portrait
their sparkling eyes are wet
so wet that once again the ideals become clear
hopes are fasten in sheaves by laboured palms
in a sensory cry of pain, despair and hope
Heaven emanates power
to the branches when they become buds again

to the buds when they become flowers
to the flowers when they become butterflies
to butterflies when they become wings
to wings when they become graceful jewels
and they will carry the vestige of my piety
like a tearful swim, *Ode to Joy*,
when You invite me, when You insist
to write with my every Sunday honesty
when I am the one who writes to You
about the crowd's heartbeat
confessing that we together have escaped
from an anonymous letter
to another down ...
so we could to be the winners

Michael Ray

Michael Ray was born in Braintree, England. He is a graduate of NCAD with a Master's in Glass. His poems have been anthologised, most recently in *The Best New British and Irish Poetry 2018*, and have appeared in *The Moth, The Shop, SouthWord, The Stinging Fly, Magma, The Well Review, The North* and *New Coin*. He has read at a number of literary events including the Cork International Poetry Festival.

A visitor

Perhaps these tides loosened me;
perhaps I've forgotten the art
of navigation and all this staring has turned
my eyes milky.
    It's an afternoon of sand –
the ocean has almost gone –
just a thin blue line below the clouds
and circle-making herring gulls.
      Worms
are throwing up lassos
beside the carnage of whelk
and mussel shells.
    Later,
when water fills these broken homes,
I'll take my boat,
row out above the wreck, lift and bait
and lower pots.
    Yesterday,
a conger, knotted,

fat as a neck;
he dropped from the pot, all teeth
and prehistory, undid himself
grinningly on the deck.
                              Just visiting
he said, making coils that seemed to have
no ends; his body spoke of wanting
home, escape
from this foreign place.
                              I steered,
with an oar, the blunt white limb,
back towards the sea,
tuning as I did, my voice to his.

Antlers

I'm viewing the 10,000-year-old elk fished up
from Lough Neagh on some good-news site,
trying to imagine how a creature could carry
such a weight. As I stare at this great rack
laid out on the fisherman's lawn, I know
I've seen these shapes before, spiralling
across another sky. And the black box, deep
inside its mud-filled skull, is still transmitting
clues to its demise. Perhaps it knew extinction
loomed, and so the creature waded out to write
its own conclusion. I return to the feed – news
folded over news, like the folds in the flag
of my insane country, its doom-laden weight
rendered unreadable by the teeming departures.

Foreign rain

Remember Laurentia, those tectonic shilly-shallies – you shifting
from the Eastern Seaboard? The way you left, quiet in the dark,
moving like a death. No stars tonight but here we are, still close,
still breathing. Sometimes, Ireland, in estuaries, when I've gone
out to sit below a pier, the sand and mud of you just lies there like
a dog that's lost. This year I let your freeze knee me through to
March; I sucked on ice, drew frost from cliffs, practised haruspicy
on your metamorphic folds, and even though you refused to
reciprocate my kisses, I fell again for your frozen beauty, from
what and where you came. And now, each evening as you undress,
reveal your gloomy secrets, I see you sideways glancing east as if
it's still the twentieth century. So, Ireland, while I wash up and
you lose yourself again in kneeling, let's remember, we're both
replenished by this foreign rain.

Opening a field

There is no refuge here from water, only a hope
that I can steer it underground.
While I work the field

I'm back in yesterday, passing flooded farmland,
chatting to the chemist on the train
about where she once lived, how her people

held the Tigris back to irrigate their crops.
She mentioned her research
with nano magnets – particles dropped into a stream

of blood, to swim through the body
for a hundred thousand miles
and, like bombs, attach themselves to terrorists.

We talked about Cessair –

Noah's granddaughter, Ireland's first woman,
how, according to the monks,
she sailed here with a small wooden god, rope

of red hair just like the chemist's, and a husband,
Fintan, who, through some strange
illuminated technology, transformed into a salmon.

And on landing, Cessair heard birdsong –
first time since leaving Mesopotamia –
that ancient place where Iraq now lies.

I fill my trench with stones, hoping
for a solution, like her,
the Iraqi chemist, her dream of asylum.

Still life

Upstairs in this makeshift gallery
the carcass of a pram
on perished tyres, body filled
with red-eyed potatoes.
Beside the pram, a leaking mattress.
Feathers, lifted by the breeze
float between open sash
and sill, settle on the wooden floor
like snow. Outside, fat
grey clouds mop up the sea.
Like cells, tiny stone-walled
fields surround this place, leave
little room to dig or plant,
bury even the smallest thing.

No place home

African sun, everyone out, smiling, the street,
cooking brooms, wicker-ware.
                              Queueing for fuel,
an eel of cars coils around the block;
even bicycles; on the handlebars, jerry-cans
pendulum.
              Men work the line with nets
of oranges, wiper-blades, avocados.
                                    Slow-time nurtures.
The queue relaxes beside hand-painted signs –
Best tobacco dust, Bee removals,
No Fear Tree-Fella.
                      Everywhere, the must of traffic,
lines of dusty metal bottles waiting
to be gassed.
              Jacaranda flowers unknot themselves,
parachute like mauve aureoles,
simmer in the tar.
                  Another brimming tank –
the dirty yellow pick-up coughs
as it rolls from the pump, the world applauded
by the family in the back, happy with nothing
but each other.

              Harare airport:
the man with no right hand helps stow
his wife's vertigo; *Tsion*, gold-winged, immaculate,
hovers, glides, hovers, counting, smiling
in seven languages.
                    The priest accelerates,
nose pressed to the glass; he rises
like steam, like a boy wanting to believe cloud
can connect continents.
                        Chicken, white rice
stars; a dimmed hum – night's cocoon.

                                        The fall
towards Dublin, dawn; the man of god
rotates, like secret switches, his gold rings,
dispenses blessings in the aisle while queueing
to receive the rain.
                        The aquarium, a queue
for non EU, the man with no right hand,
swallows; behind,
the silver glint of rising, falling fish.
                                    Cases croon,
canvas holdalls, shiny, blue, bulge like painful
sacs, and everyone, bent into their phones,
evaporates.

Natasha Remoundou

Natasha (Anastasia) Remoundou was born and raised in Athens, Greece. She is a literary scholar and activist and has taught English Literature, Drama, and Philosophy in various academic posts, as an Assistant Professor of English Literature at Qatar University, and at the National University of Ireland, Galway where she is currently a Visiting Research Fellow. Her poems written in Greek have appeared in *Melodia* magazine, *The Anthology of Young Greek Poets* in 2001. She is the mother of four children and has been living in Ireland since 2003.

The Dialect of Water

Apolis

I was told the country I'm looking for does not exist.
They insisted I spell its name, I write it down in syllables,
and looked at me like I had not two but three heads.
They asked me to find it on the map, on the globe, on Google
because no one had ever heard of it.

With a formal complaint, they unanimously accused me:
Delusional
Fraud
Stranger.

I was told mine was a futile pilgrimage
on the orbit of a bare geography
my world, an expired passport,
my oyster,

untranslatable my origins.
Exiled in homecomings,
I invent homelands
deported to the Arcadia within me.

A History of Orbits

Astonishing the vernacular of seas, miles, borders.
And look how the lateral highways of anonymous people merge,
bodies roaming to bypass customary destinations.
In Athens and in Dublin, Rory Gallagher sounds exactly the same,
and we, in a kindred odyssey,
must have learnt the sign language of memory by heart.

You, a young boy, getting ready for school.
In your bag with the harp on the front you carry a Gaelic football
and blank notebooks to learn how to write the alphabet of rhyming
        non-regrets.

And me, too, a little girl
with shoes two-sizes bigger the innocence,
I store scars and stories for you to listen to and, in translating them,
hush.

Here, at the geographical point where our circumnavigations
        intersect,
the monument of everything.

34,361+

The children dive from the Aegean's pink rocks into the
water. One or two of them – the best swimmers –
with an amphibian dip emerge onto the surface carrying in their

144

gasps as many pebbles as they can salvage from the uncertain
direction of the ascent, and strange pearls from the melanoid
bellies of sea urchins they steal with their teeth to offer them to
their sunburnt mothers.

With their amateur acrobatics – and mostly with the thorns – they
could have driven them mad if they, eclipsed behind sunglasses
with distorted mirror lenses, had not slumbered.

And just like this, and while the summer reverie and the games
mainly in a deliberate lethargy were plunging us, we lingered with a
question under the sun: that is, were the ruins on the sea bottom of
their cacti palms the most unusual objects we had ever seen, or was
it the beast that cried out foreign names and surnames and with a
paralysed oar inscribed them on the concrete sand?

    ** The figure 34,361 refers to the number of documented deaths of refugees and migrants
    due to the restrictive policies of 'Fortress Europe' as documented by the United Nations
    as of 5 May, 2018.*

Sure, it'll be grand

It's raining again.
Croagh Patrick that has vanished surrendered to the January mist,
the red trees that keep secrets deep inside their roots,
and the silent lakes in front of the aged bachelors' houses
reflecting in the water the houses and the slow breaths of the horses,
the same cities on the same roads,
and the same cemeteries with the Celtic crosses,
the butchers'
the hairdressers'
the pubs
the petrol stations
the schools with the children in uniforms
we leave behind.

With the speed of the Liffey, the Shannon, and the Moy
we reach the sea. It's grand.

Of all the things we live,
nothing would hurt more
than to lose these mornings of ours.

Random Ode

I spent the whole summer waiting for the weather to get worse.
On Grafton Street I noticed every single passer-by who looked foreign
wondering if they could tell I was one of them,
whether they know where I'm from,
if I have good English
if I have friends.

And with all these futile thoughts, I found myself sitting on the
    park bench
with a bouquet of withered tulips in one hand and the stroller in
    the other
showing you the ducks on the lake
beside a group of tourists first time in *Dublino-ma-che-bello*
and the students with beers and cigarettes and snogs,
until the tables turned and I became a duck
and you, too, a duckling
and as synchronised swimmers along with our feathered comrades,
Quackquackquack, we now speak the same language.

Bog Archives

Last night I dreamt that you existed. You brought me a
    Connemara nettle that could keep secrets, and I believed it
    and I believed you.
And all this episode must have lasted for a century because when I
    woke up I was homeless,
I had wrinkles and white hair, and I could not remember my
    name but only yours.

On seeing a lost friend at the Luas

I'd have taken a taxi had I known it.
At the Consolation Station you got in the tram
and sat beside the lady with the red sunglasses
and before I had time to wish I was the one wearing them or that
    I were invisible
or seated somewhere else that would prevent us from looking at
    each other straight in the eyes,
a whole decade elapsed since the time we became absent from each
    other's lives
and I only managed to gesture a 'hello' the same time you said, I
    think, 'oh'
and another voice announced 'Next stop Let Go Station' and I was
    relieved
because it would be worthless to add anything more to our
    primordial dialogue
just a hello and an oh, no goodbye, how are you?, long time no see.
we got lost, you look the same, what did I do to you?
and I am out, in a hurry among people in haste
held up by a young couple kissing like there's no tomorrow
and I want to tell them what will happen next
but I am already in the park and it is Friday night after ten

Dublin is a bride, I am lost in the crowd
and in my pocket I have five euros and an expired ticket.

CV

Once, I was the strangest little girl in the neighbourhood,
wearing white leather brogues mama got me for Easter
straight fringes I cut myself
and an invisible cross on the chest.

Habitus

If I had a home I'd build it from bulletproof glass and confessions.
I'd crush the roof so that I stand hospitable to snow,
in the sitting room I'd lease an amusement park,
a Museum of Complaint Letters I'd launch in the hallway,
and in the freezer I would preserve bombs and oxygen containers
to treat uninvited visitors during Lent.
I'd scout for housemates strictly bearing migratory birds' names
And a nursery with views to fields of turf and wild thyme I'd show off,
Saint Patrick, the Mediterranean, and you,
Frames on the floor I'd nail,
If I had you.

The Love Song of P.J. Kelly

In capital cities you walk, a silent soldier shielded with a brief-
case carrying files enclosing plans to impress sharks in dull
meetings, you crave promotions and brood desires of inadequate

wages, in double-breasted suits, striped ties, and winged running shoes for fast flights in competitive life championships you rest your ice gaze and forget it on cracked mobile phone screens.

At the umbilical junction between Dame Street and Church Lane, you pass by a homeless couple lying on damp blankets holding cardboards you are illiterate to interpret and walk on ignoring even Molly Malone's curves.

Outside 'The Dingle', you traverse 'The Rocky Road' through the whiskey-soaked breath of a white-bearded man and stumble upon cheerful Trinity students mumbling something about a concert at Whelan's on Tuesday night, – where the girls are so pretty – then pave your way against a folk-sea of more strangers in Leprechaun hats rushing in the opposite direction for an ambulance interrupts the robotic course of the crowd with the woollen coats, Magritte outside the Polish barber's.

It seems an obvious emergency to stand still for a moment on the two opposite banks, the ones here and the others there, and allow the hurried vehicle to parade someone's need in a rally race but there's no time to think about a stranger's pain transferred to safety or to casualty.

Until the blaring fades away behind the Georgian skyline at the far end of Nassau Street, and you remember her crying inside your parked car last summer in Elly Bay, but now you know you have been fooled again by the urban sirens, because you are already running late for office hours, the doctor's appointment, Ithaca and someone who stumbled over someone else's foot by mistake was heard whispering 'sorry' in front of Wilde's statue.

A Woe in Three Acts

I wish I'd never held the empty nest and the wings you left in
my hands, because since then, every time a finch lands on my
balcony, I think you're back home.

Athens, Iota

There used to be an ancient olive tree
right in the centre of our childhood bedroom
between my bed and that of my brother.
Its roots cracked the polished parquet
allowing meanwhile tiny proud cyclamens to grow from the cracks.

We used to climb on that tree
– its branches could hold an elephant –
and stand there playing rock, scissors, paper
until we were called to grow up
and raced to the veranda
giggling, stumbling, hungry.

I still hide a broken branch in my hand.

translated from the Greek by the author

Milena Rytelewska

Milena Rytelewska was born in Poland. Her mother is Polish, her father Laotian. She studied History of Art and Literary Arts in Jagiellonian University in Cracov. In 2018 she moved to Dublin. She is a member of the Irish Writers Centre's New Irish Communities group. She writes poetry and plays. In 2019 she performed a poem on RTÉ's *Poetry Programme*. Occasionally she is a painter.

Foreigner

I don't fit here. And I don't fit
anywhere. I'm a foreigner.

My pupils are foreign. They don't fit
my eyelashes.
My eyelashes are foreign. They don't fit
my eyebrows.
My eyes are foreign. They don't fit
my face. My face is
foreign.

My nails are foreign. They scratch me.
My teeth are foreign. They bite me.
My language is foreign. It lies
in foreign words.

The lie doesn't fit God, whom I don't
believe in.
God doesn't fit me.

My skin is foreign. It doesn't fit
my muscles. My muscles are
foreign. They don't fit my blood.

My blood is foreign. It doesn't fit
my heart.

My heart is foreign.

First Trip. Drunk Ferry.

I quarrelled with the floor. It looked at me strangely,
so I smashed it until only bloody pulp was left. And, at last, it
knows that my first name is First Commodore John Barry,
my second name is Master Mariner Robert Halpin, and
my third name is Captain Nemo (and, sometimes, you can
call me Christopher Columbus – I must tell you about that day
when I discovered America). Such a storm! Everything is
shaking. Nobody will hurt me – because nobody catch me.

It's so cold.
And so dark.
Don't go away.
Please, stay there and just let me suppress all of these divisions
and levels (I lie even about really liking this state of levitation).
Oh, look, my compass points to Time Warp.

Attention, Earth on the horizon! – you scream.
And you know that I will smash my head again.

Simone Sav

Simone Sav hails from Romania, where she completed a BA Honours in French and Literature and a Masters in Linguistics. She has been a guest on RTÉ's *Poetry Programme* and her work has been published in several magazines and anthologies.

The Song of the Bird that Does Not Belong

Perched on top of a tiller
it took a side glance at me.
Nothing was stirring the Canal,
and the echo of my footsteps on the pathway
had long since died.

I leaned in –
three shadows ruled over the dark water:
a boat, a woman and a bird –
none willing to break the silent song
of those who travel far
to find their home.

What got left behind

The last kiss of the land
my forebears tilled and cared for;
the orchard of spring toils

which blossom into the harvest of fall;
the cattle, yoke, plough, sprinkling of seed
that give way to
stacks of wheat,
baskets of plenty,
barrels of pickled hope
to make it through the winter.

What got left behind
will amount to a handful of cinders,
but only when I am gone.
For now, the memory of
a kiss, an orchard, wheat and cattle
carry me through dawns and sunsets
on this foreign land.

If Insults Were for Sale

It's rare I wake at break of day and drag my 'undeserving
    migrant' self
out of the comfort of my bed
to queue for insults.
But today I sip a hot drink, spread my marmalade,
put clothes on, make-up on my 'foreign' face
and hurry down for a fresh batch of insolence
and vile abuse.
No more of these pre-made, fast-insults that come pre-packaged
    and half price.

At length, I see the shuttered blinds of the *Insult Shop* –
and in front of it, a queue of eager clients, waiting
to replenish their supplies with the latest invectives.
Three biddies are the first in line, with woven bags, ugly, unadorned.

I recognise a politician in full-blown campaign, whose face
crowns the top of every other pole in town;
he is carrying an empty box of 'Subtle Slander' –
an expensive range of poisonous affronts
which, as the label says, 'Can easily be passed off as harmless
banter.'
A famous salt-and-pepper poet tries to hide beneath a rather
large hat,
ashamed that the muse of witty criticism failed her yet again.

Within minutes, hurried figures join the queue.
Unlike them, I am utterly selfish –
they want to gift their insults to others …
I want them all for myself.

If people cannot look at me, see past skin-deep and weight-large
traits
and love me for who I have become in this adopted country,
I'll take the second-best thing – I'll take their insults, generic
though they may be.
But once in a while, I will come down to the *Insult Shop* at the
break of dawn
and queue for the insults that can only stem from love.

Irish Mass

People step away quietly from the worn pews
shaking the dust off their knees.
The aging priest has finished his monotone blessing.
A string of pearly haired seniors are queuing
to receive the Eucharist.
They are the religious *arrière-garde* –

the last of a generation to know how to translate
the myriad of gestures, symbols and words
into a national legacy.

A grandfather stretches one cupped hand to the priest
in green garments and receives nourishment for his soul –
the flattened body of Christ in a coin-sized wafer –
light, bland and odourless.
The other holds the delicate wrist of a four-year-old girl
in a red jacket.
She lifts her open fist in innocent expectancy –
but no gift is given.

Above the altar, the statue of the suspended Christ
echoes the Rabbi's prophetic words:
'*Suffer little children …*'

Mass has ended – people step away again from the worn pews,
queuing to leave the sanctuary where the suspended Christ
cannot stretch his hands towards the disappointed child.
His palms are both nailed to the cross.
Suffering the believers.

The Present

I have a dilemma:
I set out to buy a present
for the person I hate most.
But I don't know what to get her.
She's into mind games and crafted slander
But I don't think they sell these
In the local gift shop.
Those I asked for advice thought it was a joke.

Or madness. We make a habit of celebrating
People who have shaped our lives through love,
But what about those who made us better
By standing opposite us in hatred or contempt?

I set out to buy a present for my nemesis
And I found it tucked away in a small antique parlour.
At first it didn't call out to me until I looked closer
And saw the portrait of a strong woman.

I set out to buy a present and I did.
I got her a mirror.

Eduard Schmidt-Zorner

Born in German and a 'proud Irish citizen' for more than 25 years, Eduard Schmidt-Zorner is an artist, translator and writer of poetry, crime novels and short stories as well as haibun, tanka and haiku in four languages: English, French, Spanish and German. He is a member of four writers' groups and has been published in many anthologies and journals, both in Ireland and abroad.

Uncompleted CV of a Migrant

The snail is carrying her house on the back
moving from A to B in slow motion,
a straight line, no diversion.
My line, though, was never straight.

Inquisitiveness of official questionnaires
asked for details.
I offered locations unfit for official forms.
Where born, Parents, Education, Town,
Residence Permit, Vaccinations, Driving Licence, yes or no?

Yes, born in an unprecedented winter,
where the freezing were starving
and the starving were freezing
in borrowed beds.

Packed suitcases, no address.
Ice flowers on the window,
a dead cat in a ruined house.

Where were you born? Not enough space in the form.
Pure coincidence the answer … too long a word.

Locations hesitantly spelling.
Gdańsk, Wiślinka, Wrzeszcz.
Proof of evidence: Please *x* the appropriate box(es)!
A snail has a house … *we* found a shelter
in a rat-infested cellar.

Nationality … asks the form. When? Why?
(a snail has no nationality
only leaves a shiny trace of monotony).
As a yet unborn traveller, I crossed the lands:
Pomerania, Saxony, Kashubia …
under Russian hands.

Parents had to wait four years for passports.
Nationality then: wanderer between destroyed towns.
Eternal transit, a life-long journey,
restlessly roaming with uncompleted forms in hand.

Penitential wanderings and odysseys, as the fate
of Saint Brendan demonstrated
to end where *he* started: in Ireland.

Céad Míle Fáilte, a successful marketing trick
to lure people, who come but go and do not stay.
'I hope they do not stay,'
I heard so often, 'they take our jobs away.'

Got citizenship after five years of good behaviour.
Integrated, assimilated,
pretended once to be Irish, on an art poster
and the word was deleted with a black marker …
Imposter, I was told, the new nationality.

Evgeny Shtorn

Evgeny Shtorn, MA in Sociology, is a LGBT activist, organiser and researcher from Russia. In 2018, he was forced to leave Russia and claim asylum. Currently works as Cultural Diversity Researcher at Create – National Development Agency for Collaborative Arts. He uses 'different forms of expression including poetry and anthropological diary to reflect social and political reality that makes people resist and never give up, despite the fact that everything is designed to oppress them'.

from **Translating Myself**

The rain in Dublin
is so quiet
so harmless
so tired of itself
that it sometimes seems
a morning tear
that falls
not of sadness
nor of joy
but because this is how the eye wakes up

The rain is
one of the few things in Dublin
that does not need improvement
it is how it is
does not wet much
it is very polite

cleans the streets
and goes away
like that Pole
or Brazilian
who came here
to make a living
and has stayed to live

***

Wherever you are
you will be alone
stay in solitude
feel a deep absence of
company

Although everyone listens to you
although everyone pays attention to you
although everyone
worries about you

Don't be afraid my friend
listen to this unknown accent
like music by Eric Satie
like a sad melody
like
a happy sound
of understanding
and welcome

I do not write in Russian
because I'm not able
without this healthy distance
that offers me a language
loved and alien

learned and forgotten,
but preserved somewhere
for this useless foolish occasion
to express what I feel
here and now

Wherever I am
I will be lonely
stay in solitude
enjoy a deep absence
of company

Author's note: both poems were initially written in Spanish, my first foreign language, as a way to say goodbye to it, while I was submerging myself in English. And both texts were my first self-translations into English with generous proofreading from Sarah Clancy.

Dorina Şişu

Dorina Şişu was born in Romania in 1971, but since 2011 lives in Dublin. She is a graduate of the Faculty of Philology in Brasov. She writes poetry and prose, being published in numerous magazines in Romania and abroad. She has published three poetry and three prose books, and is included in nine previous anthologies. She is one of the founders of *Itaca* magazine, a publication for Romanian writers from abroad

Today you go again ...

today you go again where you went yesterday
hear again what you've heard before
put up again with what you've put up with before
laugh unconsciously or instinctively, but maybe you don't like
    laughing
nor flaunting your breasts in a low-cut dress
you don't like red nail polish
nor high heels
you cry both what you cried and did not cry about before
you add another wound
put a cent in your hidden box
apply expired hair colour on the tired green walnut hair
add a new potato to the boil
and suffer
suffer the memories of your unjust childhood
that you scrubbed the floor with the brush
that you boiled water in a 5 kilo pot every night
that you went early in the morning to wait a whole day

for the gas tank
that you got pushed and shoved at the same queue for meat,
    oil or sugar
you remember the good icecream
you remember the first time you got beaten
when that guy came up to you and said something bad about you
your mom or your dad
your sister or your brother
you wanted to hit him but couldn't
you got punched in the stomach instead
you fell, breathless, down in the dust
 you tried to breathe, to get up, but damn, you couldn't,
why didn't you try to be worse than the one who hit you?
because you were something else
a stranger
a weirdo
you were the kid with no brothers
you were the orphan
you were the kid who spent their holidays at the communist queues
you were the kid who fell asleep saying the little angel prayer
because you were hungry
because you were longing
because you were not ashamed to be, not to be, not to have or to
    have more than you could bear
like that, in your torn clothes
like that, in your cold nights

... today you go again where you went yesterday without realising
    you've already reached the end

let's say

let's say that we are calm not desperate
that we are loving not exasperated

let's say there's no racket on the streets
but rather harp music sung to the gods
and we are so pure that we can hear it
let's say nobody died from old age
nor from hunger or during wars
let's say we forgot what I have written above
and now we are merely some lunatics smiling broadly
we open our arms and sing something like the music of the '70s
and when we get tired of so much smiling
singing
kissing
dancing
loving
we get a bottle of liquor
we take it to our mouths and keep swallowing until our tongues
feel numb
we tiptoe
and pick a red apple from an apple tree full of apples
we eat it to the core and graciously throw away the rest over the
mayor's high fence

let's say you finished reading all the lines above
you get out of bed and tear the newspaper
break the TV set
get your feet in seawater after you drove smiling to it
then you go collect the money won at the national lottery
you get yourself a house
a cat
a dog
you fix the four bedrooms
you put a table and an umbrella in the backyard
you lie down on a chair and admire the walls
until you realise that you have never realised before
how much empty space there is between the hedge and the
parking spot

on the coast of Ireland

your hobnail boots
were paired up with the lady's shoes
the skirt you asked me about is in the walnut wardrobe
and the three green walnuts
the ones you gave me in front of the church
when I was seven
I left them under God's chair

the world is changing on the west coast
what was there becomes what is here
spring hid all its cherry blossoms inside my eyes
you don't want to ask about what I won't answer
and look how the bells toll:
for life
for love
for death
for war
… you roll your eyes and don't ignore the abyss of promises
you kick virtue in the butt
and laugh – because you're not the stoic kind
and run – because you don't know how to fight
and you add another mask over your tired eyes
to create a great passing

I took one step too many on the coast
the ocean hugged my temples and we both fell silent

all poems translated from the Romanian by Aurelia Niculescu

Csilla Toldy

Csilla Toldy was born in Budapest. She escaped from socialist Hungary in 1981. For the next three years she lived in many European countries, studying and working as a translator in Germany, and now lives in Rostrevor at Carlingford Lough. With her film scripts she has received the Katapult Prize and the Hartley-Merrill Prize of the Motion Pictures Association. She works as a poet, writer and tutor of creative writing, teaching and writing about yoga and meditation.

Flotsam memories

for my father who complains about losing his own

Did I even thank you for taking me to the sea? You set me afloat
    on a voyage,
not knowing that I'd wash ashore here, at the end, on the *real*
    edge of the continent.

I woke early with excitement, ran to check the colour of the
    Black Sea, to play
with the cyan waves 'touch or die', the drama of my life.
    Collecting shells,
I found a wobbly piece of ice that was in fact a jelly fish, *stranded,*
    perhaps even dead.
I jumped on it. My bare jelly feet slipped.

I had no sea vocabulary; knew nothing about seaweed, sea
    urchin, cove or lagoon;
I was wordless like a baby, squealing with joy.

The next time it was the Baltic. Angry waves threw our boat
    around on our way
to the point where WWII began near Danzig. A drunken
    woman with a broken arm
told me all her sorrows in Polish, what important message in
    those haunted eyes,
I had no idea, but she would not let go of my hand.

A year on Adriatic brine burnt my wounds after crossing the
    border near Trieste.
The pain signalised freedom, the bruises of birth, I suppose,
    wrapped in azure.

When we reached the Channel in Normandy, Calais was empty
    of refugees then,
we were the only ones on the shore, in an old converted VW,
    gazing at periwinkle
clouds perched on the edge of the continent. I admired the teal
    statues by Rodin,
the long rolling waves matched the incoming cumulus from the west.

After many years without the sea I had a glimpse of thick algae
    in Venice.
Later in Split, still before the war, we swam naked and baked
    under the sun.
The salt was sharper than any sweat or tear. Our skin burnt
    senseless.
Even smiling became a naturist move, a two-act slow-motion
    ballet.

Back inland, cogged into dry industrial city life, I forgot the sea
till it tinted my toes verdigris, on a sunny day in Brighton.

Looking from this edge of the world, it's 'snot-green' and mirky,
but the people are vibrant. Deep silence cradles our stories.

Ives Klein dabs the night-sky in winter, and makes a sea-bed
for Aurora Borealis, seeping into the cracks.

Here, too, we beach comb, hunt for whale sperm or vomit –
   ambergris –
while seals watch us from afar, and love is graceful but shapeless.

Eriko Tsugawa-Madden

Eriko Tsugawa-Madden is from Hokkaido in Northern Japan and has lived in Dublin since 1989. Shortlisted for the Hennessy Awards in 2003, her work has been included in *Poetry Ireland Review* and *The Stinging Fly* and in the Dedalus Press anthology *Landing Places* (2010). *Bride of the Wind*, a bilingual book of her poetry in English and Japanese, was published in 2013 by Kinseido Press.

Page Turner

Each time I reach the last line
My mother's hand turns the page like a score turner.
I stop reading and watch an old freckled hand.
The blue veins raised through the thinned skin,
Branching out until they fade away.
The knuckles, stiff and bent like a snake slough.
Familiar terrain.
These are my hands but so often
I can't tell these from my dead mother's.
She comes back to turn the page for me.

Apache

Frank, my neighbour said he was an Apache.
He came here from Arizona and his American post box says
    'Native',

It shows the profile of an Apache in full headdress.
He is the only Apache I know, so far.

His small dog barks like mad each time I pass.
One day this big man came out to see.

I asked him the name of the dog.
'He is Tyson, I am Frank.'

Frank introduced himself as an Apache.
My Japanese hand was swallowed by his in our handshake.

His mother was an Apache, his father was an Apache and
His grandparents were all Apache.

Frank's wife is Irish and
Tyson of unknown type, still barks like mad.

Fr. Bradley

Walking along the long corridor,
On the way to the dining room in Dalgan House
Fr. Bradley asked 'What is corridor in Japanese? '
'Roka' said I.
'Oh, yes. Oh, yes. I have forgotten almost all my Japanese.
It is amazing how quickly it slips away.'
Walking along the corridor, he must have been thinking
Of the Japanese word for everything he saw,
Stairs, windows, walls, floor, ceiling, and corridor …

We lunched alone in an enormous empty dining room.
He asked me if I want consommé or potage.
'Consommé,' said I.

'So do I, consommé is much better.'
He seemed pleased with my choice.
We sipped it, sitting across the table from each other.
He asked me if I could say 'London'.
My tongue staggered in my mouth not to say 'Rondon'.
'L ... L ... London.'
'Not bad,' he said.
He seemed content I had managed to pronounce the 'L' almost.
Next time when I visited, he neither asked me questions
Nor spoke at all from his sick-bed.
His deep-set eyes wide open, looking fixedly at the ceiling.

Sitting beside his bed, I remembered he had said
All the people he knew as a young man were long dead
When he finally came back to Ireland, like Oisín.

When I whispered 'Sayonara, Fr. Bradley' in his ear,
The eyes swiftly blinked a few times.
His response to my goodbye.

Mother died yesterday

My mother died yesterday
This month of October, five years ago.
It was early in the morning.

She was brought to my sister's house and laid out there.
That night I went to mother's house with
A can of beer and drank it alone.

Then I opened the fridge looking for more beer or anything.
It was full with food.
She could have lived another week without shopping.

I ate some pickles
Some out-of-date yogurt
A spoonful, another spoonful.

Mother died yesterday,
This month of October, five years ago.
That night I laid myself out on her old bed.
My first time home in four years.

Bogusia Wardein

Bogusia Wardein was born in Wroclaw, Poland but her literary home is Galway. Her first published poem was nominated for the Forward Prize in 2013. Since then fifty of her poems have appeared in print publications internationally, including the Bloodaxe Books anthology *Hallelujah for 50 ft Women*. In 2018 she won the New Zealand Poetry Society International Competition and performed her work at the Edinburgh Fringe Festival. Find her at *bogusiawardein.com*

From the West Coast

It's Arthur's day, and night. The weather here is impermanent.
What they call a glorious day is only a glorious split second.
Umbrellas are useless unless you want to fly. People ask me
how I am but don't stop to listen to the answer.

They thank me at the most unexpected moments. They eat late
at night and wonder why they get beer bellies. After drinking
they mark their territory by spewing here and there. *Aggression
and verbal abuse towards staff of the Emergency Department
isn't tolerated.*

The paper says males here are among the ugliest in the world,
just behind the Poles. And they are short. For ten lines of
a recommendation letter by Doctor Fahy I will have to sleep
with him once, for fifteen I must sleep with him twice.
People call towers castles, hills mountains and greens parks.

Girls put headbands on their bums. Men wear sandals to match their black suits at the dinner gala. Today's lecture on art started twenty minutes later than it shoud when most people had still too arrive. The sign in a shoe shop in Abbeygate Street reads *Leather is not a waterproof material.*

Many houses don't have numbers and if it happens that they do it's difficult to locate a sign with the name of a street. There are no woods in the area. People say it's because of the English. There are only a few bus stops in the countryside. If you are lucky to find one, there is no timetable on it. Buses are delayed. This is not how I imagined my death.

I Consider My Home Planet

thanks to Christopher Smart

For it is flat and its fields are greener than Ireland.
For it is bundled up in blue skies.
For it cruises smoothly.
For its four seasons last for three months each.
For its flowers come into blossom in March.
For its women can walk alone in the woods if they wish.
For its golden hour lasts two.
For its tomatoes taste like tomatoes.
For it has masculine moons.
For everyone there gets a good night's sleep.
For it lacks antonyms for love and compassion.
For its people are not akin to wolves.

For firstly they welcome you when you leave the womb.
For secondly they help you to take first steps.
For thirdly they give you a map and compass.

For fourthly they say what they mean.
For fifthly they mean what they say.
For sixthly they do not dig pits for anyone.
For seventhly they respond to your call.
For eighthly they wait for you at the station in the cold.
For ninthly they are reliable like the standard metre in Sèvres.
For tenthly men beg you to dance with them.
For finally they serve you tea when you are old, sick or tired.

Christian Wethered

Christian Wethered was selected for the Poetry Ireland Introductions reading series in 2016. Since then he has been published in *The Moth, Poetry Ireland Review* and *Ink, Sweat and Tears*. His debut pamphlet, *I Don't Love You* (Eyewear), was shortlisted for the Melita Hume Prize.

Woodcote

I think about boarding school every day:
the people, the closeness;
how it enabled me never to grow,
just live on in that weird place –
the dormitories, the homesickness,
the long waiting and absent love
that still cared but couldn't see me;
the hours I spent alone,
asking why my parents had gone –
if they'd surprise me and come,
If I was doing well or missing
something – all this at eight.
Anyway, I can't stop thinking.
I don't want to.

Bray

sitting next to the sea
with scruffy hair blowing

reminds me of hairdryers
at school the massive ones
the matrons held while we
stood in a line waiting for
hot air to blow down our necks
our hardening towels
smelling of each other

You Were Born in an Ark

You were born in an ark
and the animals were as many as you could name
while waves chopped below
and we swayed with the winds.
All the while you slept as though
the rocking were internal, warm,
and you smiled inside.
Below animals stood to protect
us from the sea; and we were so safe
under the balsa bow,
the stern ahead, when Noah
cocked his head to see.
And when his dove flew in
we rejoiced – you felt
a kind of surge, like running,
but so still, and your mother smiled.
I loved the animals, erect, noble –
protected by their flesh;
they would have died for you.
When the ship docked
you were a tiny red thing;
we kissed you on the head
and started again

Landa Wo

Landa Wo is a poet from Angola, Cabinda and France. His work has previously appeared in *Cultura , Cyphers, Nashville Review, Poetry New Zealand, Scrivener Creative Review, The Penny Dreadful* and elsewhere. Selected by Roddy Doyle as the winner of the 2007 Metro Éireann writing competition, he has won a number of awards including the Éist poetry competition and the Féile Filíochta international poetry competition.

On the hill, my tomb, marine cemetery

On the hill, my tomb, marine cemetery
Hidden in the mountain. Ghost-ancestors.
Writing worn off the tombs – second death.
We believe we live in the heart of the living.
They die in their turn. First death.
I am the marine cemetery of another.
The sea rejects the bodies.
I recite the names of the disappeared
My sorrow dries in the sun of forgetting.
Life resumes its course.
Without me.

Nidhi Zak/Aria Eipe

Nidhi Zak/Aria Eipe is a poet, pacifist and fabulist. An Indian-born Irish resident – via Egypt, France, New Zealand, Norway, Oman, Poland, Qatar, United Arab Emirates and those United States – her work appears in literary journals including *Banshee, B O D Y, Poetry Ireland Review, Rattle, Splonk* and in *The Irish Times*. She was awarded an inaugural Ireland Chair of Poetry Student Prize in 2019 and Jaipur Literature Festival's First Book Club Award 2018.

Tres(s)pass

ammachi taught me how to kiss / my small face in her hands / bony cheekblade whetting mine / breathing in sharp / lungfilled as if she had / just been born and I / so close / enough to smell / giddy heat / oiled ringlets / like coconut / like matriarch / tough brown outside / tender white inside / so

later / when he put his tongue / down my throat / I gave it back / because a man / who doesn't know / how to kiss you / doesn't deserve to / touch your hair.

Hard Border

So much talk of backstops and borders
bad politics heralding a return
to a history no one wants to see
repeated

so they tell us stories
instead: so many urban legends
         that are probably untrue

like, have you heard the one about the house
   in Pettigo, partitioned through the middle,

or the Belfast woman shoving butter down her socks
the brainy British official beckoning her near
     for a friendly fireside chat, all that offending
         sticky yellow warm pissing past her legs

or the crafty fisherfellow on that disputed estuary
        between Donegal and Derry,

who painted his vessel two conflicting colours
so he could fish in the liminal lake without a fig for quotas,
   buzzing busy as a worker bee between both harbours

or the bold schoolboy on his bicycle
     pedaling across each day
customs guards turning his pockets inside out,
        their notions upside down,

finding nothing,
     until lines were lifted,
checkpoints closed, guns given up,

then they asked him what it was,
the precious cargo he'd been smuggling
          all those years

– they thought he'd never come around,
   and he said, like any boy that age –
         bicycles

because what could we love

> any more
> than the things which give us wings?

Ama de Casa

The year my family moved to Santa Fe, New Mexico crowned
the bizcochito the official State cookie. Doula Maria, our new
nanny, took it upon herself to show us how to bake the aromatic
cinnamon-anise sensation. Doula spoke English in an accent
so luxurious, it made you want to roll in it like a dog in fresh-
mown grass. She chattered incessantly about Chiapas, telling
stories of her childhood home, the cocky-rooster backyard, the
chicken-scratched patch. Everyone became an accomplice to
her liaison with language: *Amor, como se dice, how you say*, she
would sidle up to us shyly, grabbing at her Tzeltal twins – Chico
and Ines – scampering in and out of the open kitchen door,
hair like the glossy rumps of corvids seated astride their heads.
In the hollowed-pumpkin flicker-haze of that first Halloween
night, they weaved their way between the rest of us baking skull-
shaped bizcochitos for trick-or-treaters; punching them out in
pairs – icing those mocking eye sockets, those grin-and-bear-it
teeth – showering them with sugar like a blessing. *Espera, hijos!*
she begged but the dusty diction of Inglés held no hope for
the young, they resisted like revolutionaries: Spanish like a sea
bird darting, thieving, glimmers of foreign fish in their wide-
mouthed glee.

C'est poésie

Dublin airport
            arrivals
I wait

     for the person who does not come
     each time the sidewide jaws of frosted glass
                        glide open

standing by a generic café chain where sparrows
make a home
         flitting low
from the place where, earlier,
     rafters would have been,

man coming through with a boy I assume
is his son, tired
           both of them wanting
             to be elsewhere,
breathing different air,

but when he sees a bird, his eyes fill with wonder

l'oiseau!   he points out to the child,
l'oiseau!   but this boy
            cannot see bird,
cannot see life hopping across hard tiles,
hiding among the cheap legs
of chairs manufactured in China;

man hunched now on haunches, eyes
     level with the boy's, bright,
pointing with extended finger:

     l'oiseau! regardez! là-bas —

183

and in this moment, I am back in Paris,
giving my French viva at La Sorbonne,
with Mme. Houillihan's bejewelled hands

pointing to a page in a picture book,
                              a scene
               of domestic contentment:

a mother in the kitchen, a sous-chef daughter
a father with his feet up in front of the telly
and two boys playing
               with remote controlled cars in the hall.

She taps one manicured fingernail
on the girl's hair – *regardez-vous*,
her grey-eyed gaze prods me for the word:

oiseau, I say,
               then again,
willing the word to mean the thing
that she wants me to name,
                              but it isn't –

it's *cheveux*,
and I will continue to confuse
these two, long after I have left
               France

and am no longer forced to prove
               that I know
               what I'm talking about
or fudge my way through the intricacies of a foreign tongue;

when I'll be able to buy things
               that cost more than thirty euros

because I won't feel ashamed
                    of not knowing higher numbers

and when passers-by ask for the time,
I will be able to tell them
                    down to the minute,
not rounded off to the hour, or half,

but right now she is waiting
                              impatiently
for me to get it
                    right
                              and I don't

so I point out the things I do know
                              in lieu:

                    la fourchette, les oeufs, la poubelle,
        and wonder idly why the French
        gave dustbins such a pretty-sounding name.

She snaps the book shut, says *bien,*
asks me, for the final part,
        to make sentences
            out of certain verbs,
                    first – *aimer,* to love.

            J'aime.   I tell her.

            She waits.

I sit there.   And we wait.

She makes a forward motion

with her hand, I say *c'est tout,*

she shakes her coiffed head no:

Aimer quelque chose ou aimer quelqu'un,
bien sûr! Mais j'aime, seulement,
                                        n'existe pas
                    ce n'est pas possible,

            – earrings shaking –

c'est la même chose en anglais,

she finishes   defiant.

                            But it isn't.

Because in English, I can say 'I love'.

Because love can stand
            on its own –
                        what else is there?

Oh là, c'est poésie! she laughs,
batting the flawed thought away,

inquisitive bird hovering around
                            her fingers
                                fringed with emeralds.

Dedalus Press

Established in 1985, and named for James Joyce's
literary alter ego, Dedalus Press is one of Ireland's
longest running and best-known literary imprints,
dedicated to contemporary Irish poetry and poetry
from around the world in English translation.

For more information, or to purchase copies of this or
other Dedalus Press titles,
visit us at **www.dedaluspress.com**.

*"One of the most outward-looking
poetry presses in Ireland and the UK"*
—UNESCO.org